HOW NATIONS
GROW RICH

HOW NATIONS GROW RICH

The Case for Free Trade

Melvyn Krauss

New York   Oxford
OXFORD UNIVERSITY PRESS
1997

Oxford University Press

Oxford   New York
Athens   Auckland   Bangkok   Bogotá   Bombay
Buenos Aires   Calcutta   Cape Town   Dar es Salaam
Delhi   Florence   Hong Kong   Istanbul   Karachi
Kuala Lumpur   Madras   Madrid   Melbourne
Mexico City   Nairobi   Paris   Singapore
Taipei   Tokyo   Toronto

and associated companies
Berlin   Ibadan

Published by Oxford University Press, Inc.
198 Madison Avenue, New York, New York 10016

Oxford is a registered trademark of Oxford University Press

Library of Congress Cataloging-in-Publication Data
Krauss, Melvyn B.
How nations grow rich : the case for free trade / by Melvyn B. Krauss
p.   cm. Includes bibliographical references and index.
ISBN 0-19-511237-7
1. Protectionism.   2. Welfare state.   3. International trade.
I. Title.
HF1713.K732   1997
382'.73—DC20   96–32434
CIP
Rev.

1 3 5 7 9 8 6 4 2

Printed in the United States of America
on acid-free paper

To Rufus
1982–1994

A good boy, a true friend, and a real character.

Contents

Preface

I wrote *How Nations Grow Rich* to synthesize, extend, and apply the themes and analysis of three other of my books—*The New Protectionism* (published in 1978), *Development Without Aid* (published in 1983), and *How NATO Weakens the West* (published in 1986). The book was written while in residence at the Hoover Institution at Stanford University. John Raisian, the Hoover director, deserves the special and sincere thanks I publicly offer him for maintaining an atmosphere of unparalleled academic freedom and excellence at Hoover. There is no better place to do academic research than at the Hoover Institution. This book is but one small product of Hoover's stimulating environment.

The John M. Olin Foundation has been a long time friend of the Hoover Institution, and it has been my friend as well. The foundation is led by one of the great U.S. Treasury Secretaries ever, The Honorable William E. Simon, and I have indeed been fortunate to benefit from the Secretary's expert advice, counsel, and support. Bill Simon gave me the confidence and wherewithal to put pen to paper. For this, I am extremely grateful. I am also indebted to Olin's executive director James Piereson for his extensive help.

As always, I have benefitted substantially from conversations, comments, and criticisms of my Hoover colleagues. Henry S. Rowen has been particularly helpful. We at Hoover are lucky to have a stimulating colleague like Harry. Bruce Bueno de Mesquita had some interesting thoughts on the futility of trade sanctions. Needless to say, I stole unashamedly from Bruce. Professor Edward Tower of Duke University, as referee for this book, also made some very good points that I have incorporated into the work. I hope he does not mind.

Larry Mone, the president of the Manhattan Institute, has helped me disseminate the book's ideas to the general public. I am extremely grateful to him for this. My collaboration with the Manhattan Institute goes back to 1978 when the Institute was known as the International Center for Economic Policy Study (ICEPS). Their very first book, before their George Gilder and Charles Murray salad days, was my *The New Protectionism*. I am proud of my long association with this fine institution.

Finally, I am grateful to my wife for putting up with me.

November 20, 1996   *M.K.*

Introduction

There can be no doubt that the prosperity of the industrial nations since World War II has been due largely to global specialization and interdependence. No single country does all tasks today—products are designed in one country, produced in another, and assembled in a third. But the increased standard of living that has resulted from this global specialization and interdependence, based on comparative advantage and liberal international exchange, has led to a growth of the modern welfare state. This includes an increased demand for economic security, and social measures which guarantee politically-determined minimum consumption standards for citizens, environmentalism, and consumerism.

There is no inherent reason why the growth of the welfare state in the Western industrial countries should conflict with the process of global specialization and interdependence—that is, there is no inherent reason for the welfare state to be protectionist. But as the debate over the North American Free Trade Area (NAFTA), the General Agreement of Tariffs and Trade (GATT) and the recently established the World Trade Organization have demonstrated, today's welfare state has evolved into a protectionist state. U.S. consumer advocates, such as Ralph Nadar, see free trade as a threat of consumerist legislation; U.S. environmentalists, such as Jerry Brown, see free trade as a threat to environmental legislation, and so forth. For no valid reason, the modern welfare state and the process of global specialization and interdependence have been put on a collision course.

The source of the gain in living standards from international exchange is the so-called law of comparative advantage, explained in my first chapter, "The Advantages of Comparative Advantage." Specialization and interdependence through international exchange increase the average productivity of the nation's productive resources by reallocating or transferring them from lower- to higher-productivity uses. Free trade does not create jobs as is sometimes mistakenly alleged by free trade advocates—it creates income for the community by reallocating jobs and capital from lower-productivity to higher productivity sectors of the economy. The gains from trade are the gains from a more efficient allocation of the nation's productive resources.

When nations trade with one another, the value of their imports do not necessarily equal the values of their exports. Countries such as Japan that have relatively high savings rates and export capital have trade surpluses. Countries like the United States that have relatively low savings rates and import capital have trade deficits. It is generally thought that a trade surplus reflects a healthier economy than a trade deficit. This is not necessarily the case. Trade deficits can reflect a healthy situation and trade surpluses an unhealthy one. The particular circumstances of the trade imbalance is much more important than the imbalance itself.

This is not how the public sees it, however. Manipulated by protectionists, the U.S. public is convinced that trade surpluses are good in and of themselves and that, in particular, Japan's constant trade surplus with the United States is disadvantageous to this country and unfair. In his first term in office, U.S. President Bill Clinton used this mistaken view to pursue a protectionist policy of export promotion in the Japanese market. Clinton and his economic team insisted that Japan purchase fixed amounts of specific U.S. exports—computers, auto parts, automobiles, film—regardless of their price and regardless of their quality. Otherwise, Japanese goods would be blocked from the U.S. market. The story of Bill Clinton's "affirmative action" trade policy is told in my second chapter. The American president's reputation as a free trader comes from his support of the North American Free Trade Area and GATT—not his policies towards Japan.

Many Americans believe Japan has a trade surplus because it blocks entry of U.S. goods into its market while the United States follows free trade. This view is mistaken, not only because it identifies the cause of the U.S.-Japan trade imbalance (Japanese protectionism), but because it implies an inappropriate equity standard for a market economy. In a free market economy, the private consumer, and not the producer and not the government, is king. Accordingly, a consumer-based equity standard is the only relevant one. What the "fair trade" protectionist entreaty translates as when a consumer rather than producer-based equity standard is used is the transparently nonsensical proposition that because foreign counties damage their consumers by foolish protectionist measures, equity demands the United States follow suit! What the public must realize is that free trade is fair trade to those whom it counts the most to be fair to—the U.S. consumer.

The "fair trade" argument for protection is but one of several false arguments for protection exposed in the my third chapter. Here is a brief sampling of other false arguments for protection: (1) the cheap labor fallacy—that the advanced industrial countries cannot compete with cheap foreign labor; (2) the unemployment fallacy—that free trade creates unemployment; (3) the infant industry argument—that certain new industries which show promise of future competitiveness on world markets should be protected in their early noncompetitive stages to insure their short-run survival; (4) the neomercantilistic trade surplus fallacy—that protectionism is good because it promotes a balance of trade surplus; (5) and the cheap foreign currency argument—that protection is necessary to counter the alleged competitive disadvantage imposed on domestic producers by countries with "cheap" currencies.

Chapter Four, "Free Trade and the Welfare State," exposes an entirely new class of false arguments for trade protection related to the growth of the modern welfare state in advanced industrial countries. Ralph Nadar consumerists see free trade as a threat to U.S. consumerist legislation. Jerry Brown environmentalists see free trade as a threat to U.S. environmental legislation. Anna Quindlin human rights advocates see free trade as a threat to human rights in some of our trading partners. Pete Wilson nativists see migrants as a threat to the fiscal solvency of California's welfare state. I call the coalition of these special interest groups "the new protectionists." Their arguments are as fallacious as the traditional arguments for protection exposed in Chapter Three.

Not only has the modern welfare state given birth to new pressures for protection, it also has given new impetus for foreign aid. Foreign aid and trade protectionism are more closely related than commonly understood. Western Europe gives substantial foreign aid to Eastern Europe. Why? Because the European Union restricts the entry of Eastern European goods (agriculture and industrial) into the Common Market. To avoid a potential flood of Eastern migrants who can't sell goods in the West, Western governments give foreign aid. Remove the protectionism and the aid will disappear with it.

The futility of foreign aid is detailed in my fifth chapter, "No Cheers for Foreign Aid." Not only does the aid very seldom get through to the poor for whom it is alleged to be intended, but by subsidizing policy mistakes by recipient governments, aid often prolongs and exacerbates the poverty itself. The analysis documents that giving or increasing aid often delays the implementation of needed reforms in poorer countries, while suspending or reducing aid leads to more rapid implementation. Russia is a case in point. The West has given Russia hundreds of millions of dollars in aid. But instead of increasing the pace of needed economic reforms in Russia, the pace has slackened.

The fact that bad economic policies (often supported by foreign aid) are responsible for bad economic performance raises the question of why there are bad policies in the first place. The damage socialistic thinking and fallacies have done to the poorer countries is obvious. Import substitution and big government tax and spending policies have proved ruinous to these countries. Yet these are the very policies so-called "experts" promised the poor would lead them out of their poverty. "The LDC's [less-developed countries] are caught in a vicious circle of poverty," wrote the young Walter Heller in 1964. "To break out of this circle, apart from foreign aid, calls for vigorous taxation and government development programs; on this point expert opinion is nearing a consensus."[1]

Indeed it was—and my, how things have changed. As my sixth chapter, "The Consensus of Expert Opinion" documents, more than thirty years after Heller wrote these words, the pendulum has swung a full one hundred eighty degrees in the opposite direction. Today, virtually all scholars and statesmen—even those on the left—support a smaller role for the state in the development process than thirty years ago. And the reason has less to do with ideology than economic performance. "Development has worked above all in east Asia," writes Martin Wolf in the *Financial Times*, "[and] these countries have best conformed to the 'Washington Consensus' of fiscal conservatism, outward orientation and reliance on market forces."[2]

Today, a major threat to the economic well-being of poorer nations—whether in Eastern Europe or elsewhere—is the European Union. In my seventh and final chapter, "The Rise of Regionalism," the various ways the European Union damages the world's struggling economies are catalogued. First, there is the EU's customs union, which provides for free trade between the member countries but a common tariff against outsiders. The external tariff discriminates against the exports of the Eastern European countries, for example, even while EU officials proclaim their solidarity with their recently liberated but still poor neighbors.

The attempt by EU members to achieve monetary union also has damaged the poorer nations because of its contractionary bias. In several member countries, abnormally high rates of interest have been required to maintain their currency's fixed parity to the German Mark. The result of the high interest rates has been high unemployment and sluggish economies—which, through income effects, have reduced European imports from abroad. The additional requirement for monetary union set out in the Maastricht Treaty (that states that members reduce their fiscal deficits to three percent of the gross domestic product), only adds to EMU contractionary pressure.

Perhaps the most discriminatory and damaging policy of the European Union has been its Common Agricultural Policy. Farmers are subsidized, one way or other, in all advanced industrialized countries. But the EU has chosen the most discriminatory, trade restricting method of transferring income to farmers—import taxes and export subsidies—and this has severely impacted the poorer countries, in particular, because they have a comparative advantage in agricultural products. As Lionel Barber notes, "The lack of European leadership has created a policy toward the former communist countries which is self-centered, short-sighted and downright dangerous."A new Iron Curtain has descended upon the middle of Europe, dividing rich Western capitalist countries from their poor ex-communist cousins in the East."[3]

HOW NATIONS
GROW RICH

1

The Advantages of Comparative Advantage

The perennial issue of foreign trade policy is free trade versus protectionism. On the one side are the protectionists who in the United States today are more active and aggressive than at any time since the end of World War II. This special-interest group portrays our trading partners not as good guys who provide U.S. consumers with needed and desirable goods and services such as Honda cars, Sony television sets, etc., but as bad people who through unfair competition and dirty tricks steal jobs from U.S. workers and profits from U.S. businesses.

"Long a symbol of prosperity, free trade has become for many a symbol of poverty and treachery," writes the *Wall Street Journal*.[1] Though millions of U.S. jobs depend on international trade, the new demonizing myth holds free trade responsible for job losses and continuing economic uncertainty. In this psychodrama, Mexico stands for low-wage production that will steal jobs from Americans, and Japan stands for high-quality technology that will drive America into eclipse. The U.S. is viewed as slipping into an economic no-man's land, unable to fend off pressure from either sort of rival. As for gains by Mexico and Japan, 'there's a gut feeling that they're cheating, that it's not a square deal,' says Bill Camp, a Sacramento AFL-CIO organizer."

Standing against the special interests of trade unions and other protectionists are the free traders. Free traders argue the nation's or aggregate community's case—not special interest. They have two powerful allies on their side. One is the commonsense notion that the nation's economic well-being is measured by the standard of living of its citizens—not workers, producers, or other special-interest group. The other is the law of comparative advantage. This law states that the standard of living of the nation's citizens is higher when the nation specializes its production in certain goods, exports these goods, and imports others than when it tries to achieve self-sufficiency in all goods.

What Is Comparative Advantage?

"College instructors love to illustrate the British economist David Ricardo's insight about the gains from free trade with a story about Woodrow Wilson," writes Peter Passell in the *New York Times*. "President Wilson, they say, could type faster than his secretary. But it made sense to leave the White House correspondence to others so he could concentrate on making the world safe for democracy and other higher-productivity endeavors."[2]

In a similar vein, Paul Samuelson, in his famous textbook illustrates the law of comparative advantage by reference to the lawyer who is contemplating hiring a typist for the law office.[3] Two cases can be distinguished—that where the lawyer's typing is totally inadequate, and the so-called "President Wilson" case where the lawyer can type faster and more accurately than any professional typist who can be hired in the labor market.

In the former, the solution to the problem of whether or not to hire a typist is obvious—if a typist is needed then one must be hired. The great insight of the law of comparative advantage relates to the second case where the lawyer again is better off hiring the typist. The reason is that for the lawyer to do his or her own typing, the cost in terms of time diverted from legal work, and therefore foregone income from "exporting" legal services to others, is greater than the cost of "importing" the typing services. The lawyer makes more money by specializing in the production of legal services, exporting these services to others and importing typing services, than he or she could make by doing both tasks himself or herself.[4]

"Free trade" clearly pays for the lawyer in the above example but does it pays for the typist as well? The answer is that it most certainly does. The assumption that the lawyer is absolutely more efficient than the typist in all tasks does not mean the lawyer in fact will do all tasks. Some will be left for the less efficient partner, and this assures a market for the typist's services. The typist willingly supplies this market, specializing in typing, because alternative uses of his or her time have less economic value both to society and the typist than does typing. Free trade thus is a positive, not negative, sum game—both partners gain from it.

What both partners gain from trade, however, is income, not jobs. This distinction is not always fully appreciated, as has been made abundantly clear by the debate over the North American Free Trade Agreement (NAFTA). Former Clinton administration Labor Secretary Robert Reich writes in the *Wall Street Journal*: "World trade is not a zero-sum game in which a finite number of jobs are to be parceled out among the workers of the world. Trade is a positive-sum game in which there is no natural limit to the number of jobs that can be created."[5]

This is nonsense and betrays a fundamental misunderstanding about the nature of the gains from trade. Free trade does not create *jobs*—it creates *income* by reallocating or transferring jobs from the lower-productivity to the higher-productivity sectors of the economy. The argument for free trade—at least in the standard theory—is an efficient allocation of resources argument. Such reallocation increases income by increasing the average productivity of the nation's stock of productive resources.

Peter Passell writes: "By the rule of 'comparative advantage,' it made economic sense for Victorian England to break the political influence of its cosseted farmers by opening its borders to wheat from Central Europe and North America. That allowed entrepreneurs to focus more capital and labor on manufacturing, where it could (and did) make Britain the richest country on earth."[6]

A further caveat about free trade: claims that free trade can make both trading partners better off are not the same as claims that free trade can equalize the standard of living in both partner countries. The two are quite different. In the lawyer-typist case, for example, the lawyer enjoys a higher income, and therefore living standard, than the typist even after "free trade." The reason is that the lawyer's absolute productivity levels are higher than the typist's. Free trade makes the typist better off but it can't fully compensate for the difference in absolute productivity levels between the two. Similarly, free trade between the United States and Mexico, for instance, will not necessarily equalize the standard of living in the two countries though it will make both countries better off in terms of real income.

The Varied Forms of International Exchange

The gain from the international trade of goods and services described above is but one of several different forms of beneficial international exchange. Other forms are international capital and labor mobility.

When labor leaves a low-wage, labor-abundant economy to work where labor is scarce and wages high, for example, the world's fixed labor supply is reallocated from lower to higher productivity uses, benefiting both countries. Similarly, the reallocation of the world's fixed capital supply increases capital's average productivity because capital flows from lower to higher productivity uses. The source of the gains from international capital and labor mobility on the one hand, and international trade of goods on the other, is identical in that both involve factor reallocations (one within the economy, the other between economies) that lead to a more efficient use of the global economy's fixed endowment of capital and labor. International factor mobility and international trade are, in fact, substitutes for one another.

What are the policy implications of this substitutability? One is that a tariff on labor-intensive imports in a high-wage country can be expected to increase either capital outflow from that country, or labor inflow into the country (or both). For example, the United States presently is flooded with migrants from the Caribbean Basin. In part, this is because we restrict imports of labor-intensive products from the islands. Unable to find jobs in their own export industries, Caribbean people come to the United States to seek work. Tear down the tariff walls and the migrant flows will be reduced! Similarly, the North American Free Trade Area (NAFTA) with Mexico can be expected to cut back on Mexico's export of labor to the United States because it promises to increase U.S.–Mexican trade. By restricting trade, the tariff does not reduce international exchange—it simply causes it to take another form.

In addition to trade protectionism, labor migration to the United States also has been made excessive by the generous welfare state programs existing in certain border states. California is a leading example. Migrants to California know that in addition to whatever wage they can earn in the private sector, they also can take advantage of California's generous social services and, because many are Hispanic, can benefit from affirmative action programs as well. These artificial and unintended inducements to labor migration mean too much international exchange between the United States and Mexico takes the form of migration, and too little international trade and capital export. The most effective way to reduce excessive labor migration to California is for California to reduce its welfare state, and for the United States to follow a free trade policy. Hiring more boarder guards and building higher fences can not, and will not, stem the tide of migrants so long as quality social services and affirmative action are readily available on the U.S. side of the common border.

In Europe, the collapse of Communism has raised the specter of millions of Eastern refugees flooding the West. West Europeans want to prevent this, but they refuse to follow the requisite policies of free trade and reduction of their enticing welfare states. "A new Iron Curtain has descended upon the middle of Europe, dividing rich Western capitalist countries from their poor ex-communist cousins in the East," writes Lionel Barber in *The International Economy*. "Whether by accident or design, the EU finds itself retreating behind a Fortress Europe, restricting the flow of people, goods, services and capital between East and West. This is a travesty of the promises which European leaders and the United States were happy to insist upon in texts such as the Helsinki Act negotiated during the Cold War."[7] So long as the EU follows a "Fortress Europe" policy, the pressure for East–West migration can be expected to continue unabated.

The essential substitutability of different forms of international exchange raises an interesting general point worth highlighting. Outside the industrialized countries, there exists abundant supplies of labor—and not only unskilled labor. This abundant labor supply can not help but impact the industrialized countries either through trade flows, labor flows or capital flows. There is no way an industrialized country can—or really should—try to insulate itself from the world labor market. If the industrialized country restricts its trade with other countries, that very act stimulates increases in either labor migration, capital out-migration or both to compensate for the restrictions of trade flows. Should protection of domestic labor be rendered by restrictions of immigration, compensation takes place through either increases in trade flows, capital flows or both. Unless a so-called North Korean solution is imposed, no country can cut itself off—nor should try to cut itself off—from global labor abundancy. International exchange of whatever form is good because it ameliorates both the labor scarcity in the industrialized countries and the labor gluts in the less developed world.

Note, however, the existence of this compensation process—i.e., the substitution of one type of international exchange flow for another—does not mean protection is costless. The compensation process takes time, and the substitution may not be perfect. Until the compensation of one trade flow for another actually takes effect, protection of domestic labor can impose very real non-negligible costs on the overall economy. Moreover, certain types of flows may carry differential externalities than others. Because of the existence of welfare states, international labor flows may be a more expensive way of reaping the benefits of international exchange than, say, foreign trade flows. Following free trade is an important *safety valve* for industrialized economies that have welfare states as a permanent feature of their economic landscape.

What's So Favorable About A "Favorable" Trade Balance?

The economic argument for free trade was developed by the classical economists to criticize the mercantilistic practices of governments in the eighteenth century. The mercantilists identified a nation's wealth or well-being with its stock of precious metals. Accordingly, a country was encouraged to export more than it imported, since the net outflow of goods would be matched by an inflow of gold. To stimulate a trade surplus, mercantilists counseled tariffs and export subsidies. The tariff discouraged imports, while the export subsidy encouraged exports.

The thrust of the classical attack on mercantilism—particularly by Adam Smith in his great work *The Wealth of Nations*—was that the mercantilists incorrectly specified the wealth of nations by identifying it with the government's stock of precious metals rather than with the consumption alternatives available to the nation's citizens—that is, the nation's standard of living. While tariffs and export subsidies could increase the government's stock of precious metals, they would also reduce the economy's consumption alternatives by comparison with a policy of free trade. The classical economists argued that the latter constituted a decrease in the real wealth of the nation, even though the government's gold stock would be increased by trade interventions. Free trade is a better policy if the intent is to maximize a country's consumption opportunities.

Notwithstanding this argument, the mercantilistic fallacy that an export surplus is inherently a good thing for the nation is so ingrained in the public's mind that even today it is routinely referred to as a "favorable" balance of trade. Why should this be? Why should it be considered "favorable" to the nation if the value of the goods and services it sends to foreigners is greater than the value of the goods and services they send the nation in return?

The reason modern mercantilists give is that the trade surplus generates funds which can be invested abroad in foreign stocks, bonds, real estate, companies, etc. This accumulation of foreign assets is alleged to expand the influence and power of the surplus country, and decrease that of the deficit country, just as two hundred years ago the inflow of gold was considered to expand the influence and power of the Prince at the expense of his foreign rivals.

The current fear of and hostility to Japan in the United States, for example, is based in part on the fact that Japan's export surplus has allowed that country to build up substantial holdings of U.S. assets in what neomercantilists believe to be Japan's latest attempt to take over the world. "In recent years," writes Karen Elliott House in the *Wall Street Journal*, "all too many Americans have come to see Japan as an invincible economic machine destined to roll over the world, leaving America a second-rate global power. The sight of Japanese investors buying Rockefeller Center and Columbia Pictures, coupled with a ballooning surplus in Japan's trade with the U.S., has frightened and angered many Americans. The current best-selling novel, *Rising Sun*, panders to their fears and resentments. 'At the rate things are going, we are all going to wind up working for the Japanese', predicted Lester Thurow a few years ago."[8]

But what does it matter who owns Rockefeller Center, Columbia Pictures or whatever so long as these assets are properly managed? Japanese investors recently bought the Essex House in New York City. Do the hotel's guests really care if Japanese, Chinese, or Americans own the hotel so long as they are pleased with their rooms, service, and prices? And what reasonable objection could an American worker have to working for a Japanese boss so long as he or she paid decent wages for a decent day's work? Or would Mr. Thurow prefer working for an American who paid substandard wages? From the point of view of maximizing the U.S. living standard, what counts is how well or poorly the assets are managed, not the nationality of asset ownership.

Notwithstanding these questions, neomerchantilistic warnings of an imminent Japanese takeover of the global economy at best look downright silly today given Japan¢s prolonged recession and the enormous amounts of money Japan has lost on the foreign investments neomerchantilists have most fretted about. "In the 1980s," writes David Sanger in a piece titled "Asian Money, American Fears" in the January 5th, 1997, *New York Times*, "the Asian money that fueled scores of conspiracy theories in America was all Japanese. The sale of the giant American icons—Rockefeller Center and Columbia Pictures, the Seattle Mariners and much of downton Los Angeles—gave rise to dark warnings that decisions about the country's economic future would be made in Tokyo, not New York or Washington. Exactly how this power would be exercised was always left a bit vague. Would executives at Sony kill movie scripts about the Emperor's role in World War II or about the dark side of corporate life in Japan? In the short retrospect of seven years, the questions now sound even more paranoid than they did then. The Japanese took a multibillion-dollar bath on most of their investments. . . It seems almost laughable these days to think of the United States as an imminent "techno-colony" of Tokyo, a phrase slung around with great abandon in Silicon Valley until Japan plunged into recession."

To underline the point that there is nothing *inherently* favorable about a "favorable" trade balance, the recent example of Romania is instructive. Like eighteenth-century mercantilists who wanted gold to increase their power and influence in world affairs, Romania's ex-dictator Nikolai Ceauscescu thought his influence on the world stage would grow in the 1980s if Romania accelerated the paydown of its substantial foreign debt. To the delight of its foreign bankers and consternation of its citizens, Romania generated export surpluses by barring imports and forcing exports to finance the required capital outflow. The mandated increase in domestic savings put intolerable pressure on Romania's already meager living standard and was a prime factor behind the eventual overthrow of the Ceauscescu regime and assassination of both Ceauscescu and his wife. Is it unreasonable to argue that the Romanian export surplus had disastrous consequences for both its citizens and rulers?

A corollary of the principle that a trade surplus is not inherently good is that a trade deficit is not inherently bad. To demonstrate this point, consider the case of a country that imports capital and runs a trade deficit. The nation gains from importing capital if the rate of return from the use of the imported capital exceeds its cost. Then, while present consumption remains the same, future consumption—net of interest payments to foreigners—will be greater than what would have been the case had capital not been imported. This was precisely the case of the United States for much of the nineteenth century when we experienced persistent trade deficits with the rest of the world because we had to import much of our investment capital from overseas. These trade deficits laid the basis for the highly productive American industrial economy in the twentieth century. They clearly were worthwhile.

The trade deficits of the 1980s, during the Reagan years, provide an interesting special case of the principle that trade deficits can work for the general good. U.S. defense spending was high during this period because of President Reagan's desire to face down—and close down—the Soviet Empire. The results have been more than gratifying—yet, in part, at least, the U.S. defense buildup was financed by imports of foreign savings. Clearly, the trade deficits that financed the U.S. military buildups constituted a worthwhile use of borrowed funds even if the U.S. defense buildup was not the sole cause of the demise of the Soviet state.

Imported savings, of course, can be used to finance present consumption, in which case, the trade deficits can be viewed as less benign. When savings are imported solely to increase present consumption, society passes on interest payments to future generations without a sufficient income stream from investments to support or finance them. Present consumption increases at the expense of future consumption. This probably is the case of present U.S. trade deficits, and explains why many U.S. citizens are opposed to them. Note, however, that what troubles here are considerations of intergenerational equity—shifting the burden of increased present consumption onto future generations—not vague and misleading notions of flagging U.S. power and influence, as modern mercantilists misguidedly allege. The U.S. trade deficit may be unfair to future generations, but it is not a sign of American decline.

2

Bill Clinton's "Affirmative Action" Trade Policy

In a meritocracy, the society's glittering prizes go to its glittering talents. Quotas to achieve politically correct objectives are an anathema. In the modern welfare state, however, protective quotas are omnipresent though they are not called quotas—they are called "affirmative action." Universities have "affirmative action" admission policies; businesses have "affirmative action" employment policies; and governments have "affirmative action" procurement policies. Now with Bill Clinton as president, the United States has originated an "affirmative action" trade policy.

The Clinton administration insists—indeed demands—that Japan purchase fixed amounts of specific U.S.-export goods—computers, auto parts, automobiles, etc.—regardless of their price and regardless of their quality. If the Japanese fail to comply, Clinton threatens to block entry of Japanese goods into the U.S. market. Some call Clinton's policy "managed trade"; others a "results-oriented" trade policy. What it really represents is an "affirmative action" for U.S. exports.

Clinton justifies his bully boy tactics against the Japanese on the grounds of the persistent and substantial U.S. trade deficit with Japan. "The world needs Japan and the United States to cooperate," Clinton said at his April 1993 meeting with Japan's then prime minister, Kiichi Miyazawa. "And it can only happen if we are making real progress on this trade deficit."[1]

Clinton's emphasis on the U.S.-Japan bilateral trade deficit has been judged misplaced and dangerous by economists and economic journalists alike. "Many economists would undoubtedly agree with Mr. Clinton that mega-deficits are not popular, nor easy to explain to the great majority of Americans who prefer their economics lessons in easy-to-swallow gel caps," writes Peter Passell in the *New York Times*. "But it is equally safe to say that few economists think the chronic trade deficit with Japan is a problem in itself worth much of a fuss—or, for that matter, an economic problem at all. Economists generally reject the idea that America's chronic trade deficit with the world (or Japan's chronic trade surplus) is linked to anyone's trade policy. 'America runs a deficit because Americans spend more than they produce at home,' said Gary Saxonhouse, a University of Michigan specialist in the Japanese economy. 'We make up the difference in the imports'—or at least we do as long as foreigners are willing to finance the transactions.[2]

Saxonhouse's argument, and the relationship between a nation's savings, on the one hand, and its trade balance, on the other, can be illustrated by a simple arithmetic example. Suppose a nation produces 100 dollars worth of income but spends 120 dollars. Two things are clear. First, the nation has dissavings or negative savings equal to twenty dollars. Second, net imports also must be equal to twenty dollars if the 120 dollars worth of spending is to be reconciled with the 100 dollars worth of income. How else can a nation consume more than it produces other than to import the difference? The bottom line: savings and the trade balance must be equal. The greater the savings, the greater the trade deficit.

As is apparent from the following quote, the *New York Times* editors appreciate the logic of this argument. They point out that the U.S. trade deficit with Japan is a consequence not of Japan's protectionism, but of Japan's high savings ratio by comparison with the United States:

> Longstanding trade deficits reflect insufficient saving. Americans buy more goods than they produce, importing the balance. The Japanese do the opposite: produce more than they buy, exporting what's left over. The U.S. trade deficit won't fall—regardless of what Mickey Kantor negotiates with the Japanese—until Americans save more.
>
> That's why the strategy of 'managed trade' proposed by some in the Administration won't work. Under managed trade, Washington would set numerical targets for Japanese imports of designated U.S. goods like supercomputers, telecommunications equipment and automobile parts—and retaliate if they aren't met.

But if the Japanese are forced to import more designated goods, they will—given their unchanged savings rate—compensate by exporting more or importing fewer non-designated goods (some of which would otherwise have come from the U.S.). Besides, the Japanese Government can't control how much its citizens import unless it replaces markets with Government-run cartels—a peculiar demand for the U.S. to make. [3]

Prominent *Financial Times* columnist Michael Prowse adds his voice to the chorus of Clinton critics, highlighting the inconsistency between Clinton's protectionist stance on Japan on the one hand, and his solid support for NAFTA and GATT's Uruguay Round on the other:

Mr. Clinton and his senior advisors are behaving like economic delinquents. In December, Mr. Clinton hailed the merits of the Uruguay Round, which promises to deregulate agriculture and financial services, sectors in which the United States is highly competitive. As a "new democrat" he was all for multilateral trade liberalisation under the Gatt.

Yet a mere two months later, he solemnly chastises Mr. Morihiro Hosokawa, Japan's reform-minded prime minister, for refusing to accept numerical targets for import growth in selected industrial sectors. Such targets—essentially a government commitment to reserve a portion of Japan's home market for U.S. and foreign companies—are the very antithesis of the Gatt principles that Mr. Clinton was promoting so hard last year. Perhaps Mr. Clinton is genuinely incapable of understanding the contradiction. If so, it is lamentable that economically literate senior aides—including Larry Summers at the Treasury—are so eager to play this charade.

U.S. officials, of course, sometimes claim they are not demanding numerical targets. All they want are quantitative benchmarks to judge progress in opening Japanese trade markets. This is spurious talk of medal-winning dimensions. It is not as though Japanese trade figures are a state secret: quantitative measures of progress in opening specific markets have always been readily available.

In any case, as a member of a multilateral system, the United States simply has no right to act as judge and jury on Japanese trade practices. To put U.S. behaviour in perspective, suppose France analyzed U.S. wine consumption and found an unfair bias in favour of inferior Californian brands. Would Mr. Clinton be happy if President Mitterrand unilaterally set a numerical target for increased U.S. imports of French Burgundy? Of course not: he would instantly condemn such bully-boy tactics.

The obsession with the Japanese bilateral imbalance is even more fatuous. White House talk of impenetrable barriers creates the false impression that Japan buys virtually nothing from the United States. In reality, U.S. exports to Japan were $48bn last year, making it America's second most important market. The bilateral deficit with Japan is declining relative to U.S. national income. But even if it were rising, it would signify nothing. Surely Mr. Clinton's high-powered advisers have not forgotten the very first lesson of economics: that trade is beneficial because it facilitates specialization and division of labour. The last thing we should expect or want is balanced trade between every pair of countries.[4]

If being attacked by the generally supportive *New York Times* and *Financial Times* were not enough, President Clinton's export - protectionism has suffered the further indignity of being publicly criticized by leading economists who for many years have been closely associated with the U.S. Democratic Party. In an open letter to Clinton and Japan's former prime minister, Morihira Hosokawa, at the time of their 1993 summit, twenty-five economists including Nobel Laureates Lawrence Klein, Franco Modigliani, Paul Samuelson, Robert Solow, and James Tobin advised Japan to reject "misguided" American demands for managed trade and "myopic" calls for a cut in the bilateral trade surplus. "On managed trade the group attacked 'the crude and simplistic view that Japan is importing too few manufactures owing to structural barriers which make Japan special,'" reports the *Financial Times*.[5] "'The world needs more market-based trade, governed by internationally agreed rules, not targets set by bureaucrats, politicians and self-interested complaintents from industry'."

When a Democratic president draws public fire from such members of the Party's economic elite as Professors Klein, Modigliani, Samuelson, Solow, and Tobin, you know he's doing something really bad!

How bad Clinton's "affirmative action" trade policy actually has been can be gleaned not only from its lack of support amongst the Democratic Party's economic elite, but from its results. Notwithstanding all the hoopla and spin emanating from the White House, the Japanese have not, to any noticeable degree, opened their markets to U.S. exports.

"Clinton administration officials," writes syndicated columnist Robert D. Novak, "long had claimed that Japan would either have to blink—make major concessions—or suffer punitive trade sanctions. But as everybody in the world trading community knows it was Clinton who blinked."[6] U.S. consumers suffered, on the other hand, because Clinton's policies were widely regarded to have raised the price of the yen in terms of the U.S. dollar in foreign exchange markets. Not only were Hondas, Toyotas, Mitsubishis, and Sonys made more expensive to U.S. consumers as a result of dollar depreciation, but so were the prices of substitute products made by U.S. competitors.

Perhaps the most telling cost of Clinton's failed policy of export protectionism is the damage done to U.S.-Japan relations. The Japanese may not have a good trade policy record as far as many Americans are concerned, but the palpable hostility, distrust, and contempt shown them by the Clinton team—from the president down to his subordinates—has gone well beyond the bounds of civil treatment of an ally. It would be truly amazing if the Japanese were not deeply offended. The Clinton trade war against Japan has been totally unnecessary—both the U.S. economy and U.S. exports have done quite well—and the costs of a damaged relationship with one of our most important allies surely will be with us for years to come.

3

False Arguments for Protection

Protectionists cannot take from the many to give to the few without the active complicity of government. Only government has the power to redistribute income from domestic consumers to domestic producers by restricting imports. Only government has the power to tax the general public to subside special interests.

Sometimes, protectionists and government collude in secret to accomplish their objectives. But they often operate in the open—not only in full public view but sometimes even with the public's willful compliance.

Confusion, ignorance, and apathy are the reasons victims cooperate with their victimizers. Protectionists are master spinmeisters. Like magicians, they possess a varied bag of tricks to fool the public. A recent favorite is to argue that free trade is beneficial only if our trading partners play by the same rules we do.

This argument—that equity demands the United States protect its producers when foreign countries protect theirs—has a certain appeal but is nonetheless fallacious. Free trade is fair trade to those whom it counts the most to be fair to—the domestic consumer. When U.S. protectionists, for example, argue that it is not fair for the United States to give Japanese exporters free access to the U.S. market when Japan does not reciprocate, they use the wrong equity standard. A consumer-based standard is the only relevant equity standard in our free-enterprise economy. In a free market economy, the consumer is king, not the producer or the government.

What the "fair trade" protectionist entreaty comes down to when the appropriate consumer-based equity standard is used is the transparently nonsensical proposition that because foreign countries damage their consumers by protectionist measures, equity demands the United States follow suit.

Listen to what Milton Friedman has to say on this subject. "An argument for protection that was made by Alexander Hamilton and continues to be repeated down to the present," writes Friedman, "is that free trade would be fine if all other countries practiced free trade but that so long as they do not, the United States cannot afford to. This argument has no validity whatsoever, either in principle or in practice. Other countries that impose restrictions on international trade do hurt us. But they also hurt themselves. . . . [I]f we impose restrictions in turn, we simply add to the harm to ourselves and also harm them as well. Competition in masochism and sadism is hardly a prescription for sensible international economic policy! Far from leading to a reduction in restrictions by other countries, this kind of retaliatory action simply leads to further restrictions."[1]

James Bovard writes "'Fair trade' is one of the great intellectual frauds of the twentieth century. The louder politicians have demanded fair trade, the more trade policies have become a travesty of fairness."

Who's Dumping on Whom?

"What would you rather be," asks Milton Friedman, "a dumper or a dumpee? A dumper is someone who sells something below cost. A dumpee is somebody who buys something below cost."[2] Even a child knows it's better to buy than sell below cost. Yet fair traders and the U.S. government claim that it's "unfair" to us when foreigners sell their good to us at below-cost prices.

The big lie protectionists tell about dumping is that foreigners sell below cost only to drive out domestic competitors. Once this is accomplished, they argue, the price will be increased to make back all the lost money, and then some. Beware the Trojan horse of dumping, American consumers are warned, for it will turn its head and bite you where it hurts most—in your pocketbook.

What can one do about a big lie but expose and denounce it? Even if foreign miscreants wish to put domestic competitors out of business and raise prices to profit-gouging levels, what prevents the advent of new domestic competitors on the scene who hope to share in the foreigner's monopoly profits but through the new competition actually serve to reduce profits to more competitive levels? More dumping, perhaps—followed by more new entrants, and so the process goes on? Clearly, the only way foreigners can permanently suppress domestic competition is for them to permanently sell below costs. This is hardly likely. Still, if foreigners are foolish (or generous) enough to permanently send us "foreign aid" in the form of subsidized prices, should we not accept? After all, hasn't the United States given enough foreign aid to others over the past decades?

Once the equivalency of dumping with foreign aid is understood, it is clear who the biggest dumper on the world scene is today—the U.S. government! "When we sell wheat to India at a zero price," writes Friedman, "we are surely selling wheat below cost. That's the extreme of dumping. The only way you could go farther is by paying people to take it off your hands. All foreign aid is a form of dumping. When we give foreigners money to buy American goods, we are dumping because we are permitting them to buy things below cost. If Japan or other countries subsidize exports, they're engaging in reverse foreign aid."[3]

True dumping, of course, is rare—firms, after all, are in business to make, not lose, money. But judging from the plethora of dumping cases brought before the U.S. Commerce Department, one could think dumping is all foreigners do. Clearly, the U.S. has been using foreign dumping as an excuse for the protectionist imposition of anti-dumping duties. "Complaining about the unfairness of foreigners," writes J. Michael Finger, "has become the most popular way for an industry seeking protection from imports to make its case to the government."[4]

The sad truth is that in these protectionist times for a foreign firm to be accused of dumping in the United States is tantamount to its being convicted of the so-called offense. This is why the anti-dumping duty has become the weapon of choice for U.S. protectionists. Trade expert James Bovard estimates that over ninety percent of dumping cases brought by U.S. companies before the Commerce Department results in the imposition of so-called "countervailing duties" against alleged offenders. "Dumping," writes Bovard, "supposedly means that a foreign company is selling a product in the United States for less than in its home market, or less than its cost of production. But in the past nineteen years, Congress and federal bureaucrats have repeatedly stretched the definition. Commerce now routinely finds *ninety-seven percent* of all foreign companies it investigates guilty of dumping."[5]

A particularly grievous instance of the Commerce Department's protectionist use of U.S. dumping laws occurred in June 1993 when Commerce imposed dumping duties of up to 109 percent on steel imports from nineteen nations, as well as subsidy penalties of up to seventy-three percent on steel from twelve nations. In these cases, as usual, the Commerce Department found all foreign companies it investigated guilty of unfair trade. "The punitive dumping rates— and the likelihood of a *de facto* embargo on many types and qualities of imported steel—are the largest trade policy failures yet for the Clinton administration," writes Bovard. "Steel-using industries employ thirty times more Americans than do domestic steel manu- facturers—yet the Commerce Department seems to care only about steel producers. This dumping investigation was controlled by career bureaucrats who are widely perceived to be 'captured' by domestic steel producers. . . . The Commerce Department apparently believes that fairness should have nothing to do with how it administers America's 'fair trade' laws. Yesterday's ruling is further proof that the U.S. dumping law is one of the greatest threats to U.S. manufacturing competitiveness."[6]

From the foregoing discussions, it may appear that it is only in commodity markets that the claim of dumping has been used as a pretext for protection. But this is not the case. Dumping also has been used to justify protection in labor markets where trade unions seek to protect domestic workers from the competition of foreign workers.

Germany provides a vivid example of an advanced industrial country where government officials and trade-union leaders charge "wage dumping" in an attempt to protect artificially high German wages from the competition of foreign workers willing to work for less. To circumvent government laws and regulations that put Ger- man wages up to job-destroying levels, many German employers employ foreign workers who work for lower wages. "'Posted workers' [are] technically employed in another EU state and then posted to work in Germany," writes Wolfgang Munchau in the *Financial Times*. "Posted workers are particularly common on building sites, where they work at half the prevailing wage levels, a practice known as 'wage dumping' in Germany. . . . German politicians and trade unionists argue that the same work should carry the same wage and have raised the alarm. Bonn has reacted with a law to protect German workers against wage dumping, but the law has loopholes and its effectiveness will depend on agreement for a minimum wage."[7]

From this report, it is clear that German trade unions seek to shield domestic workers from the effects of competition from foreign workers by subjecting foreigners to minimum wage laws. "To keep foreign immigrants away for good, IG Bau (the German building workers trade union) proposes a high hourly minimum wage of DM19.54, close enough to the lowest wage band for German-resident workers," writes the *Financial Times* reporter. "The employers started off with an offer of DM15 and have since moved up to DM17. The difference does not seem large, but both sides find it difficult to cut a deal. The union argues that each D-Mark down means tens of thousands of jobs lost to foreigners. The employers say each D-Mark up means hundreds of bankruptcies."[8]

One might ask: Could there be a more vivid example of the anti-competitive, trade-restrictive purposes of minimum-wage laws than this? Minimum-wage laws have less to do with "social justice" than trade-union-friendly politicians would have us believe. On the contrary, the purpose of these laws often is to limit competition to protect the artificial, privileged positions of certain favored workers in the domestic economy from the competition of the less-favored. The bottom-line cost to Germany of the minimum-wage laws is the loss of social product that results from the "hundreds of bankruptcies" that will be induced by the artificially high wages.

The Cheap Labor Fallacy

While fair-trade arguments for protection currently are in fashion (presumably because they work so well), the classic false argument for protection is the cheap labor fallacy. The cheap labor argument is that the advanced industrial countries cannot compete against cheap foreign labor—hence, the alleged need for protection. Critics of the North American Free Trade Agreement (NAFTA), for example, base their opposition to the trade pact with Mexico partly on the grounds that American labor cannot compete with cheap Mexican labor.

NAFTA critics do have a point. High-cost *unskilled* American labor cannot compete with low-cost *unskilled* Mexican labor. But what the NAFTA critics miss is that this actually helps, not hurts, the American economy. The reason is that the U.S.-Mexican labor cost disparity forces a beneficial reallocation of American labor from lower to higher skill tasks. Reconsider the lawyer-typist illustration of the law of comparative advantage. The lawyer in the illustration is capable of doing both high-skill and low-skill tasks. The reason he or she can concentrate completely on the law, however, is the availability of low-skilled labor abroad—i.e., the opportunity to hire a typist. The lawyer would be worse off if typists for hire did not exist.

Similarly, it is the availability of cheap foreign labor that allows advanced industrial economies like the United States to concentrate its production on high-skill goods—i.e. goods which use relatively large proportions of skilled relative to unskilled labor in their productive processes—and trade these goods for imports of low-skill goods—i.e. goods which use relatively large proportions of unskilled relative to skilled labor in their production. As the *New York Times* correctly points out to its readers: "The purpose of trade is not to raise unemployment or to rack up [trade] surpluses. Its purpose is to steer workers into high-productivity jobs: into computer and software production and out of textiles."[9] The reason this "steering process" through trade works is precisely because high-cost unskilled American labor cannot survive competition with lower-cost substitutes from abroad.

NAFTA critics like Ross Perot and Pat Buchanan make a mistake when they argue that the flight of U.S. firms to Mexico to take advantage of cheap wages is a bad thing for the U.S. economy. The export of low-skill jobs to Mexico can be expected to raise, not lower, U.S. national income, because it is a part of the re-distribution of jobs within the United States from low to higher productivity uses implicit in the movement to freer trade with Mexico. What Perot, Buchanan, and other NAFTA critics fail to appreciate is that balancing the export of low-skill jobs to Mexico will be an increase in U.S. high-skill jobs emanating from the increased export of high-skill goods also to Mexico. NAFTA critics give the false impression that the trade agreement with Mexico destroys jobs, because they look at only one side—the job-loss side—of the two-sided job redistribution process.

The Unemployment Fallacy

There are two versions of the unemployment fallacy for protection. One is that protectionism creates employment—the other is that free trade creates unemployment. Both equate to the same thing— and both are examples of bad economics.

Of course, trade restrictions like tariffs and import quotas *can* increase employment *in the protected industry.* This is not disputed. But unless the employment gains come out of previously unemployed resources, increases in employment in the protected industry must come at the expense of employment decreases elsewhere in the economy. Like free trade, trade restrictions do not create jobs—they redistribute them. But unlike free trade, national income is reduced by protection, because the job redistribution process takes workers out of higher productivity and puts them into lower-productivity uses—i.e. out of computer and software production and into textiles.

Import restrictions even can destroy jobs in the protecting country if they are imposed on imports that serve as inputs in the production of other goods. Protection makes the output of the protected sector more expensive. This must have a contradictory effect on outputs—and therefore factor employments—of other domestically produced goods that use the protected output as an input in their own productive processes. Again, the employment gains in the one industry are matched by employment losses in other industries.

Protection of steel in this country is a case in point. Steel is used as an input in the productive process of goods too numerous to mention. When the price of steel goes up because of steel protection, the output of these goods must contract. Steel protection thus may increase employment in the protected steel industry but it does so at the expense of employment in other related industries.

"Alleged unfair trade cases, filed by the U.S. steel industry against nineteen countries, are casting 'a menacing shadow' over the American economy and spurring inflationary price rises, according to U.S. steel users," reports the *Financial Times*. "The users say they employ thirty times more U.S. workers than do the steel companies."[10] Milwaukee's Paper Machinery Company is an example of a U.S. firm that has been severely damaged by U.S. steel protection. "Paper Machinery, which had been successful competing against French and German companies, has had to absorb a 10–20 percent increase in steel prices since the U.S. Commerce department put temporary tariffs on steel imports," reports the *Financial Times*. "The tariffs, a result of the dozens of dumping and countervailing duty cases brought by the steel industry against companies in 21 countries, could cost hundreds more jobs in Milwaukee and other port cities and at the factories which mould steel into products for export around the world."[11]

John Norquist, mayor of Milwaukee, and a Democrat, blames both the "sheer 100 percent unalloyed greed" of the steel industry and Bill Clinton's former trade representative Mickey Kantor for the present situation. "Mickey Kantor doesn't know which products to penalize and which to subsidize," argues Norquist. "When he's trying to penalize Germany and Japan, he's hurting Milwaukee. He's decided to punish Milwaukee and punish Wisconsin to prop up this industry [steel] that doesn't want to compete in the marketplace. All they want to do is sit on their Congressmen's laps."[12]

The Milwaukee mayor is right to be fearful that firms like Paper Machinery Company might pull up stakes and take their jobs abroad to escape U.S. protectionism. There are important examples of such cases. The job losses in the U.S. computer industry in response to the 63 percent tariff placed on imports of Japanese flat-panel display screens—an input in their productive process—apparently taught Mayor Norquist a valuable lesson:

> [IBM CEO] Akers' comments, at a news conference in Tokyo, inten-sified pressure on U.S. officials to reverse a decision that was supposed to protect a nascent sector of the American computer in-dustry.... Most computer makers depend heavily on Japanese sources for their flat-panel displays, also known as liquid-crystal display screens. And manufacturers in the United States have argued that the 63 percent tariff imposed in the summer of 1991 makes their computers uncompetitive against models made in Japan.
>
> Apple Computer and the Toshiba Corporation have already begun to move their production of portable machines out of the United States (Apple went to Ireland and Toshiba to Japan), con-tending that the duty is an example of a protect-American policy that has backfired. In contrast to screens imported as components for computers assembled in this country, computer systems that already contain the screens can be shipped to the United States without the duty.[13]

Even Bush's former Commerce Secretary Robert A. Mosbacher—the party responsible for this "protect-America policy that back-fired"—(which one hasn't?)—apparently had second thoughts about the policy's wisdom. The Commerce Secretary is quoted in *Business Week* to the effect that "We're not happy with the outcome."[14] But what other outcome could there have been? Didn't Secretary Mos-bacher realize that the IBMs, Apples and Toshibas were being dam-aged by the dramatic increase in their costs imposed by the 63 percent tariff on flat-top screens? What better means was there to cir-cumvent the cost increase than by moving production facilities abroad?

To the relief of American workers who like their jobs in the computer industry, the flat-top tariff was rescinded two years after its imposition in June 1993. "The Commerce Department last week abandoned its two-year-old sixty-three percent tariff on Japanese-manufactured active-matrix liquid-crystal displays, the screens used in high-end laptop personal computers," wrote Eric J. Savitz in *Barron's Magazine.* "The decision puts an end to an ill-considered and fruitless effort to boost the struggling U.S. display industry. . . . Faced two years ago with the prospect of absorbing the government's stiff levies or, alternatively, raising the price of their wares, the PC companies did the only logical thing—they moved their laptop assembly operations offshore. 'It amounted to an eviction notice for the laptop computer manufacturers,' contends IBM spokesman Mark Holcomb. Big Blue, which originally had planned to assemble some of its laptop models at a plant in Raleigh, N.C., instead set up production in Japan. Likewise, Apple moved laptop production from Colorado to Ireland. *In short, the primary accomplishment of the tariff was to throw Americans out of work.*"[15]

How Shifty Is Labor?

Some critics of free trade argue that the theory of the gains from trade assumes factors of production to be mobile, and while this may be a reasonable approximation of reality as far as capital is concerned, labor can be "sticky" as between different skills, geographic region, employers . . ., etc. Free trade under conditions of labor immobility, it is argued, does create unemployment as jobs lost in the contracting import-substitute industries are not necessarily made up elsewhere in the economy.

This argument, it should be noted, is not really an argument solely against free trade *per se* but against all change in the economy. It implies that changes in tastes be discouraged; that no new income transfer programs be started, since these imply resource redirection; that economic growth be eliminated—in short, that all change be discouraged, because the re-allocation of resources implied by change cannot be effectuated by the economy without creating some unemployment in the process. The argument, in other words, is absurd.

Moreover, government policy itself may be the source of labor immobility, so that the argument is not against free trade but against government policies that reduce the flexibility of the domestic economy. One way welfare governments impede labor mobility, both occupational and geographic, is by social policies of extended unemployment benefits. The purpose of unemployment insurance is to help workers out during temporary periods of economic distress. But if unemployment insurance is available on an extended basis, as is the case in many welfare states, unemployment insurance *permits* the worker to resist the necessary adjustments that are called for by the economy. One such adjustment may be to leave the occupation in which he or she was previously employed. Another may be to leave

the geographic area. Here, of course, there is a real conflict between
the needs of a dynamic economy on the one hand, and the socalled
"revolution of rising entitlements on the other." The needs of the
economy dictate that workers change occupations and/or location at
the same time that the worker feels that he or she is "entitled" to
work at his or her old trade at his or her old geographic location.

More and more, workers have come to expect democratically
elected governments to secure these entitlements for them—a trend
that has already reduced the abilities of welfare economies to adjust
to the needs of a changing economic environment.

Another government policy that restricts factor mobility and
wage flexibility is the legitimization by government of labor-market
monopoly practices. The restrictive practices of trade unions clearly
constitute an ever-increasing burden on the economies of the industrialized nations. In 1995, this is all too well known, and it is not
only the extreme right that is calling for reform in this area. Perhaps
it is somewhat unorthodox to blame government for the growth of
monopoly power in factor markets. But antitrust activity has traditionally been a legitimate function of government. It is clear that the
time has come for governments to be more evenhanded in the pursuit of antitrust responsibilities. Monopoly practices by trade unions
in factor markets deserve attention at least equal to that paid monopoly practices by firms in product markets.

The Infant-Industry Argument

One of the older arguments for protection is the so-called "infant-
industry" argument—that certain new industries which show great
promise of *future* competitiveness in world markets should be
protected in their early noncompetitive stages to insure their short-
run survival.

The analogy between human and industrial development implicit in the infant-industry argument is clear. Just as humans in their
early stages need to be protected by society, so do industries.

Of course, we also know from human development that some
protected infants never grow up. This is the central issue raised by
the infant-industry argument. Does protection of an industry mute
its incentive to go through what, after all, is a painful period of
adjustment from infancy to maturity? "The infant industry argument," writes Milton Friedman, "is a smoke screen. The so-called
infants never grow up. Once imposed, tariffs are seldom eliminated.
Moreover, the argument is seldom used on behalf of true unborn

infants that might conceivably be born and survive if given temporary protection. They have no spokesmen. It is used to justify tariffs for rather aged infants that can mount political pressure."[16]

For industry to survive and prosper in today's competitive marketplace, it must be able to innovate—and government subsidy dulls the appetite for innovation. Consider the most innovative industries in this country—biotechnology, computers, micro-processing ... , etc. None received infant-industry protection during their start-up phases. All were financed by venture capital.

"The pace of computer technology change is accelerating." warns Bill Gates, chairman and cofounder of Microsoft. "Every company is going to have to avoid business as usual. The only big companies that succeed will be those that obsolete their own products before someone else does." Note what America's most successful entrepreneur does not say. He does not say: "The only big companies that succeed will have to lobby Washington for handouts."

In addition to reducing the incentive to innovate, a second flaw in the infant-industry argument for protection is its implicit assumption that government—which cannot even run the post office properly—has sufficient knowledge and insight to pick winners and avoid losers when choosing which industries to subsidize and which to ignore. The skill of picking winners and avoiding losers, after all, is so rare that the market pays those blessed with it extraordinarily high incomes. It would only be in the rarest of cases that such persons would work for government.

Infant-industry arguments for protection must be rejected therefore because (1) governments have no skill in picking winners and avoiding losers, and (2) even if they did, the effect of protection would be to rob the potentially competitive industry of its incentive to innovate. Notwithstanding these severe limitations, the infant-industry argument survives because it serves as a convenient subterfuge for governments to pass along special-interest money to favored industries, friends, and supporters.

The Neo-Mercantilist Trade Surplus Fallacy

Neomercantilists believe the sole legitimate function of trade policy is to generate a trade surplus. Trade policy is good if it lead to trade surplus, bad if it leads to a trade deficit. The reason neomercantilists worship the trade surplus is that it gives the surplus nation power to buy the real and financial assets of foreign countries.

Economists scoff at these views. Trade policy, they believe, should be geared to increasing the nation's living standard—not some vague, loosely defined concept of economic power. What good is increasing the nation's "power" over foreign assets if such increase lowers the domestic living standard? The two clearly would be in conflict if protectionist means—which most neomercantilists favor—are used to increase exports and decrease imports.

They also will be in conflict if the foreign assets purchased by the surplus country fall in value. As noted above, the Japanese trade surplus has enabled Japanese investors to buy U.S. bonds, real estate in New York, California, and Hawaii, and entertainment companies like Columbia Records. But the Japanese have taken enormous financial losses on many of these investments because they tend to buy in at the top of the market. Clearly, the Japanese living standard has suffered because of these losses. Someone ought to ask neomercantilists Clyde Prestowitz, Lester Thurow, and Chalmers Johnson: do you really believe Japan's economic power and prestige has been enhanced by the trade surpluses that financed these disadvantageous investments?

Neomercantilistic views on protection and the trade balance also should be called into question, because both theory and practice demonstrate protection has little bearing on the balance of trade.

Consider a country whose trade is balanced that imposes an import tariff. The trade balance cannot move into surplus, because domestic resources flow out of exports to "finance" import substitution. Imports fall but so do exports. In the new equilibrium with the tariff, import and exports are balanced though at lower levels than under free trade. The tariff affects the level of trade—both imports and exports are reduced—but not the trade balance.

This reasoning is based upon a simple model in which there is no saving. Once the analysis is expanded to include savings behavior, however, it can be shown that the critical determinant of the nation's trade balance is its savings rate. Countries that produce more goods than they consume—Japan not only is *an* example, it is *the* example— have a trade surplus because they export the excess of production over consumption. Countries that consume more than they produce—the United States—have a trade deficit because they import the excess.

This implies the U.S. trade deficit will not fall—regardless of the tariffs and export subsidies it may impose—unless Americans increase their savings. With unchanged savings, U.S. import restrictions, for example, only cause American consumers to compensate for the restrictions by buying more imports of nontariffed goods, or more domestically produced goods that otherwise would be exported, or both. If neomercantilists really want the United States to reduce its trade deficit, they should argue for policy changes that increase American savings. (Some have: Lester Thurow, for example, argues for a consumption tax—the value-added tax—to replace the federal income tax in part because it should increase U.S. savings.)

A related point. U.S. President Bill Clinton has made a big issue out of the U.S.-Japan trade imbalance, using it as a pretext to force the Japanese to increase their imports of U.S. goods (see Chapter 2). But if the American President really was serious about reducing the U.S. trade deficit, he would attempt to increase U.S. savings, for example, by eliminating U.S. double taxation of savings, indexing the capital-gains tax for inflation and/or reducing its rate, abandoning the corporation income tax, and substituting a flat-rate consumption tax for the personal income tax. To this point, Clinton has done none of these things.

The Cheap Foreign Currency Argument for Protection

When the Mexican peso lost 40 percent of its value against the U.S. dollar during the financial crisis of January 1995, U.S. protectionists and NAFTA critics cried foul. The devalued peso, they feared, would give Mexican producers an "unfair" competitive advantage in U.S. markets while U.S. producers suffered an "unfair" disadvantage in Mexican markets. Their response was predictable: pull the U.S. out of NAFTA.

Even neomercantilists like Perot and Buchanan could judge the peso devaluation "unfair" only if the Mexicans engineered the devaluation for reasons of the trade balance. But the peso devaluations were forced upon the Mexicans by the capital flight of worried international investors—not engineered by them to improve the balance of trade. The last thing the Mexicans wanted to do was devalue their currency.

"Mexico in the first years of the Salinas term did a fantastic job of restoring its economy by doing all the right things: reducing government spending, balancing the budget and privatizing industries," writes L. William Seidman in the *Wall Street Journal*. "World markets responded and Mexico became a member in good financial standing, able to borrow in the credit markets (particularly in the U.S. market).

"Like a kid in the candy store who suddenly has unlimited access to the open counter and grabs more than is good for him, the Mexicans took advantage of their new credit-worthiness and took on more debt than they could handle. The result was debt stomach ache from over-consumption. When the illness began to show, the markets reacted by dumping Mexican debt and pesos. Mexico responded by trying to prop up the peso and used over half of its dollar reserves before giving up the doomed effort.

"A market judgment 'mistake' had been made by investors and lenders who didn't properly evaluate the situation: The Mexicans were overdoing a good thing and had borrowed too much. This is the crux of the current problem."[17]

Capital outflow, peso devaluation, and the expected trade-deficit reduction all have conspired to bring the Mexican living standard back to earth with a thud. To argue that the Mexicans purposefully engineered the peso devaluation for neomercantilistic trade-balance reasons is worse than mistaken—it is absurd.

Notwithstanding this fact, NAFTA critics have been using Mexico's financial crisis and peso devaluation to sow doubts about the trade agreement. It is true, of course, that U.S. exports to Mexico should fall significantly in the next year both because of the peso devaluation and the economic recession in Mexico that surely will follow its financial crisis. But the reader must be clear: the U.S. stake in NAFTA is not as a beggar-my-neighbor, neomercantilistic institution to score big trade surpluses with Mexico by following a cheap-dollar–expensive-peso policy. Rather it is to improve the U.S. standard of living by reallocating U.S. resources from low- to higher-productivity uses. Protectionists in this country are against NAFTA precisely because they want to keep American workers in textiles and out of computers and software. Remember, a leading voice against NAFTA in the United States has been the U.S. textiles unions.

Trade agreements are not to be judged by the fact that one or more of the partners is prone to periods of macroeconomic instability. If that were the case, Italy would have been thrown out of the European Union long ago. Whether a trade liberalization agreement can be judged "good" or "bad" depends on its ability to provoke beneficial factor reallocations. Notwithstanding Mexico's crisis-prone economy, Mexico and the United States are a good match precisely because the trade liberalization agreement between the two is expected to provoke beneficial reallocations of labor and capital within both countries. This is a consequence of the fact that U.S. low-skilled labor cannot compete with Mexico's low-skilled labor, and Mexico's high-skilled labor cannot compete with U.S. high-skilled labor. These cost differences are the twin foundations upon which NAFTA is built. Without them, the trade agreement would be scarcely worth pursuing.

Legitimate Arguments for Protection

These are good reasons why this subsection is one of the shortest in the book. There are only two quasi-legitimate arguments for protection. National security is one, because imports of sensitive products can be cut off in times of hostilities. But the national security argument for protection is not for import restrictions—they increase the price of the imported good to consumers as well as domestic producers. Domestic production subsidies are better because they are cheaper in terms of pure resource misallocation than either tariffs and quota restrictions. Subsidies lack the consumption-cost component of import restrictions.

Like the infant-industry argument, a prime danger of the argument for national security protection is its misuse by domestic protectionists who care more for their own pocketbooks than national security. I remember when the Swedish government put a substantial tariff on shoe imports and justified the imposition on the grounds that Swedish soldiers needed shoes. This elicited a roaring good laugh from the entire Swedish nation. The likelihood that Sweden—a neutral country for as long as one can remember—would enter into hostilities with another country was about as great as it abandoning its welfare state. Swedish shoe producers also laughed—all the way to the bank.

The second quasi-legitimate argument for import restrictions is the so-called terms of trade argument. A big buyer in a market can reduce the price of the good it buys by restricting demand. A big country can reduce the price of its imports by imposing a tariff. The gain from reducing import prices—in effect, taxing foreign income—can be greater than the tariff's pure resource misallocation effect. Still, whatever gain a nation may achieve with an "optimal tariff" alternatively can be achieved by explicit transfer between the two countries at a lower resource misallocation cost to the world economy. The optimal tariff is inferior to explicit income transfer.

4

Free Trade
and the Welfare State

The modern welfare state is characterized by a large public sector and extensive government intervention into the private economy. Its purpose is to achieve a wide range of social objectives—e.g., equalization of incomes, equal access to certain goods (health care, education), environmentalism . . ., etc. Welfare-state programs are manifest in all the Western industrialized nations though they have reached their extreme in the smaller countries of Northern Europe—Sweden, Norway, Denmark, Finland, the Netherlands.

A Change of View

During the decades of the 1950s and 1960s, the welfare state and free trade were considered to be complimentary with one another. Free trade bolstered the economic base of the welfare state, which made financing its social consumption and income redistribution programs that much easier. This made sense but could not survive the 1970s. As the economic performance of the welfare state faltered, so did its commitment to free trade. Slowly but surely, the welfare state has evolved into a protectionist state.

Here are some of the ways the welfare state undermines economic performance. First, high rates of social consumption means high taxes. High taxes reduce work effort, distort investment decisions, undermine the economy's division of labor by encouraging the substitution of inefficient tax-free barter for fully taxable monetized market transactions . . . , and so on. None of these consequences of higher taxes are beneficial for the economy.[1]

Second, because labor in particular is reluctant to move, the welfare state's promise of economic and social security has meant that the factors of production are maintained in low-productivity uses, rather than being forced by the market place into higher-productivity alternatives. This lowers the average overall productivity of the economy's productive resources. Third, the equalization of wages for skilled and unskilled workers necessarily reduces the skill level, and thus productivity of the work force. And fourth, mandated labor benefits (such as health insurance) increase the cost of labor to employers. This forces labor from the more productive private sector to either the less productive public sector (if government is the employer of last resort) or unemployment.

Today, for example, artificially high labor costs and labor-market inflexibility induced by its welfare state are widely acknowledged to be major causes for current record rates of European unemployment—now running over 12 percent in some countries. "European Community officials said there was broad agreement that labor costs and rigidities must be reduced if Europe is . . . to create jobs with growth," writes Roger Cohen in the *New York Times*. "With tax and social security payments adding an average of 40 percent to labor costs in Europe, European employers have shown increasing reluctance to hire and have brought the welfare state to a point of unparalleled crisis."[2]

Rigorous scientific analysis also supports the view that high labor costs have caused high European unemployment rates. Prestigious Columbia University economist Edmund Phelps argues that "big increases in payroll and personal income taxes in most countries have been mass job-killers (In France the 10-point rise has boosted the unemployment rate by about a point and a half). . . . When businesses or workers are taxed on wages, a business must pay more to provide the same employee incentives as before, and it cannot then afford the same work force as before. Employee incentives cost business still more if taxes finance welfare entitlements that make wage earning less attractive. The rise in these two tax rates have been steepest in Canada and on the Continent. These economies also tend to show the steepest rise in unemployment—from a rate below the American one to a rate well above it."[3]

Phelps's study relates high taxes to high unemployment rates. A new study by economists Alberto Alesina and Roberto Perotti takes the analysis one step further. They relate Europe's high unemployment rate to its welfare-state income-redistribution programs. An important assumption of their analysis is that unions attempt to maintain the disposable real wage of labor.

"The basic idea of the paper is as follows," write the two economists (one from Harvard, the other from Columbia University). "An increase in, say, income taxes used to finance redistribution to retirees and/or unemployed workers induces the labor unions to increase wage pressure. This effect is magnified if the redistribution to the unemployed increases the union's reservation wage. The increased wage pressure is reflected in higher output prices and therefore induces a loss of competitiveness. In turn, the loss of competitiveness causes a reduction in the demand for exports and a fall in unemployment in the exportable sector. The same chain of events—from higher wages to higher prices and lower employment—leads to a fall in employment in the nontradable (services) sector. In fact, the price of nontradables increases even more than that of tradables because the former do not face any foreign competition."[4]

The effect any given change in income-redistribution policy has on competitiveness, according to the authors, depends on the degree of centralization of labor markets. "Intuitively," they write, "as the degree of centralization increases and the typical union becomes larger, the monopoly power of each union increases and fiscal policy becomes increasingly distortionary." European welfare states combine both centralized labor markets and substantial income transfer—thus, high European unemployment rates come as no surprise. "In a panel of 14 countries for the period 1960–1990, we find that the (empirical) results are supportive of our theory," write Alesina and Perotti. "For instance, we find that, when taxes on labor increase by 1 percent of GDP, unit labor costs in countries with an intermediate level of centralization increase by up to 3 percent relative to competitors." Given this loss of competitiveness, then, is it any wonder that protectionist pressures are growing in the European economies.?

The Road to Protection

Protectionism has been a common response to the European unemployment crisis caused by its welfare state. "'The European Union should use its new-found unity over trade to push for protection against unfair competition' ... argues France's ex-prime minister Edouard Balladur. 'All of us west Europeans ... have lived since the Renaissance, or at least since the beginning of the colonial epoch, a bit like the privileged of the world. This has enabled us to build up systems of social protection which are very necessary but very costly,' he said. . . .'Can we (west Europeans) take it for granted that we will remain sufficient leaders in a sufficient number of sectors to survive—in the face of countries with populations infinitely larger than ours and with levels of social protection infinitely smaller? I say we should leave this to the market, but only up to a certain point. What is the market? It is the law of the jungle, the law of nature. And what is civilization? It is the struggle against nature."[5]

By implying the advanced industrial economies cannot compete with poorer countries with abundant populations and meager social protection mechanisms without subsidy, the ex-prime minister of France commits the classic "cheap labor" fallacy: which sectors of a nation's economy survive and prosper, and which fail, depends on comparative advantage—not on whether it has dear labor or elaborate social defense mechanisms (See Chapter One).

Mr. Balladur is probably the last person who needs to be lectured that France's labor is dear because it is high-skilled. Indeed, France's comparative advantage—like that of the United States—lies in high-skill goods, which it exports to the poorer countries in return for imports of low-skill goods. Both France and the poorer countries benefit from this exchange. If France now were to artificially restrict imports of low-skill goods from the poorer countries, as Balladur suggests, France would wind up producing more low-skill and less high-skill goods. This hardly is the recipe knowledgeable observers would recommend for brightening the future prospects of the French economy.

While trade along comparative advantage lines clearly has benefitted France considered as an aggregate, it is true that, inside France, some groups have gained at the expense of others. For example, trade has widened the gap between the real wages of French skilled and unskilled labor (the same is true in other advanced industrial economies as well). "A widening wage gap between the skilled and unskilled is exactly what economic theory would predict," writes the *Economist* magazine. "In particular, the Stolper-Samuelson theorem (proposed in 1941 by Paul Samuelson and Wolfgang Stolper, and sometimes known as the "factor-price equalization" theorem) predicts that the removal of trade barriers will reduce the income of a factor of production, in this case low-skilled labor, that is used relatively intensively in imported goods; and it will raise the income of a factor of production, in this case high-skilled labor, that is used intensively in exports."[6] Trade should not be restricted, however, just because it causes income to be redistributed.

In the face of so-called adverse changes in the income distribution, the best way low-skill workers in industrialized countries can help themselves is to increase their skills level. Education and retraining are the only answer for unskilled workers who are dissatisfied with their present and likely future economic lot in life—though to acknowledge this is not to acknowledge a case for government subsidy. The benefits from skill upgrading flow primarily to the individual, not the community. The idea that the community must pay for the retraining of workers negatively impacted by foreign trade or other types of policy shocks implies either that somehow the community is responsible for the adverse changes, or that there is some sort of implicit contact between the state and individual which guarantees politically determined minimum-consumption levels for all citizens. These are welfare-state assumptions and are not valid for a capitalist economy. Notwithstanding this fact, the community does receive some benefits from the upgrading of worker skills, so that there may be legitimate grounds for some community support for worker retraining.

The linkage made by French ex-prime minister Balladur between "costly systems of social protection" on the one hand, and protectionism on the other—that because industrialized countries have "costly systems of social protection" they must turn to protectionism—highlights a serious dilemma for the global economy. There can be no doubt that the prosperity of the Western nations since World War II has been due in large part to specialization and interdependence. No one country does all tasks today—products are designed in one country, produced in another, and assembled in a third. But the increased income and standard of living that has resulted from this global specialization and interdependence based on comparative advantage has led, among other things, to a growth of the welfare state, including an increased demand for economic security, social measures which guarantee politically determined minimum-consumption standards for citizens, environmentalism, and consumerism.

The dilemma posed by this development is clear. Because of its evolving protectionism, the growth of the welfare state now threatens the very specialization and interdependence that is the basis for Western prosperity in the first place. The manner in which the Western industrial states resolve this dilemma to a large extent will determine their continued prosperity.

The "New Protectionists"

While the founders of the European and American welfare states may not have been hostile to free trade, their modern counterparts—environmentalists, consumer- and animal-rights groups, feminists, and trade unionists—are out-and-out protectionists. This has been made abundantly clear, first, in the debate over the North American Free Trade Agreement—which was rigorously opposed by the entire panoply of welfare interests in the United States—and again in the debate over whether the United States Congress should approve the so-called Uruguay round of trade-liberalization talks conducted under GATT auspices.

"Many of the people involved in the NAFTA battle considered the U.S.-Mexico-Canada trade agreement a part of their bigger fight against trade liberalization being negotiated during the world trade talks," writes Asra Nomani in the *Wall Street Journal*. "The NAFTA scrap may have launched a hard-core coalition against trade liberalization for the first time since the end of World War II."[7] "Thirty-five anti-NAFTA groups fired off a letter to President Clinton, warning that GATT would be a 'significant step backward'," reports *The Wall Street Journal's* "Washington Wire."[8] "While the NAFTA battle cry was 'Jobs to Mexico,' the anti-GATT complaint will be that the deal cedes power to 'faceless bureaucrats in Geneva.'"

I have christened this coalition of special-interest groups the "new protectionists," first, because it is indeed a protectionist coalition and, second, because the motivation for the coalition's opposition to free trade is protection of social legislation rather than enhancement of the profit-and-loss statement of a favored industry (traditional protectionism). For whatever reasons, U.S. consumer advocates today view free trade as a threat to consumerist legislation, environmentalists view free trade as a threat to environmentalism . . ., and so on.

A favorite target of consumer advocates is the newly established World Trade Organization (WTO). "Under the WTO [World Trade Organization]," writes Ralph Nader, "member nations can challenge each other's health and safety laws before trade tribunals in Geneva, charging that these laws are 'WTO-illegal' because their effect is to restrict trade. Since our country has numerous laws that are more protective of its citizens than those of other nations, the U.S. would be a frequent delinquent. If these unaccountable tribunals decide that our laws—for example, those limiting the use of exported nuclear materials; advancing food, air and water safety and recycling; protecting dolphins, and requiring labeling—are 'non-tariff trade barriers,' we would be obligated to repeal them or pay perpetual fines."[9]

Mr. Nader fears the WTO because he knows a good deal of consumerist legislation is indeed beggar-my-neighbor. Here is an example—cited in my 1978 book *The New Protectionism*—of how U.S. automobile-safety standards protect U.S. auto manufacturers from foreign competitors. "An example which illustrates how protection of the environment has meant protection of local enterprise is automobile safety standards in the United States. The entitlement here is that of a 'safe environment.' It is a well-known fact that America has traditionally been a big-car country, while Europe had tended toward the smaller car. With the substantial increase in the price of gasoline, small cars have become more popular in the United States. But it seems that Detroit cannot build a small car that satisfies the U.S. consumer. The Italians, however, build a very popular small car—popular in Italy and throughout Europe—the FIAT 500 and 600 models. These cars cannot be imported into the United States though, because they are not considered to be safe by the U.S. government. This is very convenient for the Detroit auto manufacturers who, judging from past experience, could not build a small car to compete with the FIAT 500. Of course, Detroit argues that the lack of popularity of American-built small cars means that Americans do not want small cars in general, rather than they just don't want the small cars that the Detroit auto makers have offered them to this point."[10]

This example is from twenty years ago. But to this day American consumers are being denied access to moderate-priced Mercedes-Benzes and BMWs widely available to Germany's middle class because these cars do not meet the U.S. Department of Transportation's safety standards and/or local fuel-efficiency standards. To make the so-called "grey-market" foreign cars legal for use in the United States requires a substantial conversion expense, particularly in California where pollution standards are extremely high. This effectively keeps them off U.S. roads. The only Mercedes-Benzes and BMWs seen here are super-expensive ones, manufactured in Germany to meet U.S. standards, and priced accordingly.

An example of a more deliberate use of health regulations for protectionist purposes comes from the Netherlands where marketing regulations prohibit corn syrup as a food additive allegedly for health reasons. The mystery of why corn syrup should be considered less healthy than sugar is solved once it is realized that, unlike producers in other countries, Dutch manufacturers of chocolate, fruit purees, pastes, jams, jellies, marmalades, . . . , etc. do not use corn syrup as an additive. They use sugar; hence, banning corn syrup effectively bans the importation into the Netherlands of foreign-made sweets and candies. Though the corn-syrup prohibition does not appear to be beggar-my-neighbor—it applies equally to domestic and foreign corn syrup—its effect is more malevolent then meets the eye.

The problem of sorting out the environmental from protectionist aspects of various pieces of social legislation clearly is a thorny one— and it was no more so than in the case of landing rights for the Concorde in New York City. When the British and French applied for landing rights for their supersonic aircraft at Kennedy Airport in the late 1970s, they were opposed by local citizens' groups in New York City who feared the noise level of the new plane. Protection of American aircraft manufacturers had nothing to do with their objections to the Anglo-French plane. But the British and the French argued the case as a straightforward protectionist issue. For them, the noise level or environmental impact of the plane simply represented a convenient excuse for U.S. protectionists to hide behind—and in the end Anglo-French arguments won the day. The Concorde has flown in and out of JFK on a daily basis now for over two decades.

Because so much of today's consumerist legislation is beggar-my-neighbor, Nader and his allies fear GATT would be what he calls a "pull down" agreement—that is, an agreement that would scale back America's welfare state. "The agreement's controlling provision," writes Nader, "is that any domestic law that affects trade in any way must be the least trade restrictive possible."[11]

But trade neutrality does not necessarily imply a pulling down or scaling back of consumerist and environmentalist legislation—only that the legislation be cleansed of its protectionist, beggar-my-neighbor attributes. For example, when the Europeans argue that a U.S. carbon tax would be a less trade-restricting way of promoting clean air than our current gas-guzzler tax and fuel-efficiency laws, they are not opposing U.S. clean air legislation *per se*. Similarly, when the Europeans favor signs in supermarkets, not disclosure on the products themselves, as a less trade-restricting way of providing U.S. consumers information on the nutritional content of food products sold in stores, they are not opposing consumers being better informed about the products they consume—only the way the information is passed onto them.

There can be no doubt that once the enforcement of international trade rules is given more teeth, domestic health and safety laws will have to be written in the least trade restricting manner as possible— and some which are not correctable may have to be repealed altogether. But this is a good thing. Ralph Nader does not want to admit it, but there are international externalities attached to a good deal of domestic health and safety laws. Other countries' trade can be damaged by them. When this occurs, mechanisms such as the World Trade Organization can be useful for reconfiguration and even elimination of the offending measures. Mr. Nader in a provocative manner calls this "Trade Uber Alles." To more measured observers, it is a necessary correction of an international external diseconomy or non-tariff barrier to trade.

The World Trade Organization got off to a good start when in its very first major ruling (Jan. 1996), it found a key section of the U.S. Clean Air Act discriminates against foreign oil refiners. Apparently, in trying to reduce air pollution in the United States, the Clean Air Act imposes tougher standards on foreign than U.S. oil refiners. This is back-door protectionism, pure and simple. The trade panel ordered the United States to develop a plan to change its rules on imported gasoline, or face trade sanctions.

The *New York Times* applauded this decision:

> The newly created World Trade Organization issued its first major ruling last week, rendering a judgment against the United States. A judicial panel ruled that a provision in the Clean Air Act discriminates against foreign oil producers, violating trade rules. Contrary to a reflexive denunciation by Pat Buchanan, the Republican Presidential candidate who charged that the ruling threatens American sovereignty, the action shows that the trade organization is off to a good start. In the long run, the W.T.O. will greatly benefit Americans.
>
> It is important to note that the W.T.O. ruled against only one part of the act and affirmed the right of the United States to protect its environment to any extent it wants, as long as the law does not favor domestic producers over foreign producers. The United States has fought hard for that principle because it protects American exporters. The panel ruled that a provision of the Clean Air Act forced foreigner oil producers to temporarily meet higher pollution standards than their American counterparts. This judgment was reasonable.[12]

Reason, however, may not be Pat Buchanan's forte. Venezuela is one of the countries that complained about the trade-restrictive effect of the Clean Air Act. "At his [Republican primary] rallies," writes James Bennet in the *New York Times*, "Mr. Buchanan says that his response to such whining would be straightforward. 'I think we tell them VENZ-oh-WAY-luh to take a hike!' "[13] The Buchanan know-nothing Right has joined the Nader antibusiness Left in an unholy crusade against free trade.

A final point. In his failed attempt to undermine the GATT agreement, Nader raised the specter of "unaccountable tribunals" and "faceless bureaucrats in Geneva" overturning U.S. domestic legislation. "Challenges would be decided by a tribunal of trade bureaucrats in Geneva," claims Public Interest, a lobbying organization founded by Nader, in a *New York Times* advertisement. "Their decision would be automatically adopted unless a UNANIMOUS vote of all 117 member nations agrees to stop it. Including the country which brought the complaint! The tribunal decisions would be made in secret. With no public participation, oversight or transcript. No conflict of interest rules. No press coverage. No outside appeal."[14]

But a *New York Times* editorial (July 23, 1994) dealt a stunning rebuke to the so-called consumer advocate:

> Mr. Nader exaggerates when he says that the dispute panels threaten to overturn local and Federal laws governing everything from the size of children's toys to nutritional labels. Countries could challenge U.S. laws as unduly restrictive of trade. But the laws cannot be overturned as long as they are based on scientific standards.
>
> Furthermore, the U.S. has so much leverage that it has little to fear from retaliation; in fact, the World Trade Organization would not change the dynamics of trade for any strong industrialized nation. Currently, the U.S. can legally block unfavorable rulings; and while complaining countries can still retaliate, they rarely do so out of fear of triggering a self-destructive trade war. The same fear would govern retaliation under the Trade Organization even though the U.S. could not resort to the legal nicety of blocking unfavorable rulings. *Indeed, the trade body could do a lot of good if its proceedings bring domestic pressure to bear on protectionist practices that reward special interests at the expense of ordinary consumers.*[15]

Free Trade and the Environment

Just as U.S. consumer advocates see free trade as a threat to consumerism, U.S. environmentalists see free trade as a threat to environmentalism. In particular, they fear free trade between countries of high and low environmental standard lowers the former to the level of the latter—i.e. that free trade makes the environmental standard in the least stringent country, the *de facto* common environmental standard for the entire free trade area. This is why many U.S. environmentalists oppose NAFTA. "The truth about NAFTA," writes environmentalist and ex-California Governor Jerry Brown, "is that it will create a race to the bottom in . . . environmental standards. This is inevitable if we rashly link ourselves to Mexico where environmental laws are unenforced."[16]

But Governor Brown and other U.S. environmentalists are wrong about the effect NAFTA is likely to have on U.S. environmental standards. Free trade between the United States and Mexico does not pressure U.S. environmental standards. Rather it causes an adjustment in the product mix of high- and low-pollution goods within each country. The country of higher standard—where the cost of pollution is dear—increases its output of low-pollution goods, and decreases its output of high-pollution goods. The country of lower environmental standard—where the cost of pollution is cheaper—increases its output of high-pollution goods, and lowers its output of low-pollution goods. Free trade causes the country of higher environmental standard to "export" its polluting industries to the country of lower standard, not lower its own environmental requirements. This is a good social result because production of high pollution goods gravitate to the country of lower environmental standard where the cost of pollution is cheaper, and vice versa.

The hostility of U.S. environmentalists to NAFTA, therefore, is misplaced. NAFTA should lead to an international *redistribution* of production such that the U.S. has fewer, and Mexico more, of high-polluting industries. The total amount or scale of global pollution, however, is more or less unaffected by free trade. This analysis is critical for public policy because it implies that:

1. High environmental standards do not necessarily place the country's domestic producers at a competitive disadvantage under free trade arrangements;
2. The benefits from free trade are independent of the level of environmental standards in the trading countries;
3. Free trade does not necessarily pressure the high-standards country to adopt the lower environmental standards of its trading partners; and
4. The argument that countries with higher environmental standards cannot pursue free trade unless its trading partners adopt equivalent standards is essentially an excuse for protectionism.

The *Financial Times* editors have it right when they write: "It is untrue that trade necessarily harms the environment, that all countries ought to have the same environmental regulations, that differences in environmental regulation are bound to create unfair competitive advantages, or even that the chief global environmental threat is posed by the development of poorer countries."[17] Environmentalism and free trade are perfectly compatible.

Free Trade and Mandated Social Benefits

The revolt against higher taxes in the welfare state, along with the need to restrain escalating budget deficits, has put enormous pressure on private firms to provide social benefits that traditionally had been the province of government. Mandated social benefits (MSBs)—health insurance, paid family leaves, consumer entitlements, etc.—have dramatically increased the cost of doing business in the welfare state. Add to MSBs the costs of complying with ever increasingly stringent environmental standards, and the incentive for private firms to flee the welfare state to more congenial locales is apparent.

Yet welfare-state firms will not easily abandon their home market unless they can freely export back to it from abroad. This is why free trade is considered critical for the escape process. It is argued that free trade allows firms to circumvent the burdensome social charges and at the same time preserve their domestic market share. The prospect of an exodus of private firms to avoid MSBs and other cost-increasing interventions can work to constrain pursuit of these policies by welfare-state governments.

The fear that Canadian firms would flee south to the United States was the precise reason Canadian socialists opposed the 1988 U.S.-Canadian free trade agreement. The principal argument was that the dismantling of protectionist barriers in Canada would force a scale back in Canadian social programs if Canadian goods were to remain competitive within the free trade area. "Critics [of the free trade agreement] argued that the deal would result in pressures on Canada's social programs being applied by Canadian businesses unable to compete with their U.S. counterparts," reported the *Globe and Mail*. "The real pressure is going to come from Canadian companies that feel they are unjustly penalized by having to pay for social programs through higher taxes to the federal and provincial governments."[18]

"NDP Leader Edward Broadbent says his rejection of the free trade pact is motivated less by its actual terms than by his fear that there will inevitably be capitalist pressure on social programs under it.... Mr. Broadbent told reporters, 'I have an immense fear that if the agreement is put in place, corporate pressure would mount to harmonize Canadian social policies, such as subsidized medicare and pensions, with lower American standards.' Mr. Broadbent indicated this would come about as a way of reducing the tax disadvantage of companies operating in Canada and competing with U.S. firms."[19]

What is not evident to welfare-state advocates like Canada's Mr. Broadbent is that their fears that free trade would pressure harmonization of social programs throughout the free trade area down to the level of the least generous partner are misplaced. It is true that in the short-run, before suitable adjustment can take place, Canadian firms would be placed at a competitive disadvantage *vis à vis* their U.S. competitors if they had to charge higher prices to their consumers to compensate for the higher taxes necessitated by Canada's more generous welfare state. But as the Canadian balance of payments moved towards deficit—and the U.S. towards surplus—because of the different tax and price levels in the two countries, either Canadian wages would fall, or the Canadian dollar would depreciate against its American counterpart, until external balance was restored. In the longer run,—i.e., after this adjustment—the competitive advantage gained by Canadian firms from the wage decrease or currency depreciation would offset the competitive disadvantage they suffer because of higher Canadian taxes. Harmonization of social programs would not be necessary because differences between countries would be adjusted by the currency exchange rate and or wage changes.[20]

Mr. Broadbent and other social democrats need to look to the experiences of the Northern European welfare states before adopting a protectionist line. In countries like Sweden, the Netherlands, and Denmark, there was a literal explosion of social-welfare programs during the 1950s and 1960s. At the same time, these small European welfare states all followed free-trade policies. The sixty-four-thousand-dollar question is this: if free trade undermines social welfare programs as critics like Mr. Broadbent allege, why did social democracy flourish in these free-trade countries during this twenty-year period? The argument that free trade is antithetical to social democracy is refuted both by economic analysis and historical experience.

European Monetary Union and the Welfare State

Rather than free trade, the biggest threat to Europe's welfare state today emanates from the continent's drive for common money or European Monetary Union (EMU). The German people are not likely to sacrifice the "hard" Deutsche Mark for the "soft" Euro (as the proposed common currency is called) unless the other EMU participants can demonstrate to German satisfaction their monetary predispositions are as anti-inflationary and hard money as the Germans'. The crucial test is the Maastricht Treaty—to participate in the EMU, budget deficits for all participants must be below three percent of GDP, and the public-debt ratio must be less than 60 percent of GDP.

At a time when all prospective EMU members—including Germany—have budget deficits well in excess of the three percent target, it is clear that the adjustment to EMU will be extremely deflationary. M.I.T. economist Rudi Dornbusch writes: "There is virtually no country with a budget that makes the Maastricht criteria, including Germany and France, the two key countries. As a result, all of Europe is plunging into budget cutting, all at once, with the likely outcome of a slowdown. True, the budget cuts are appropriate even without EMU, but their timing, size and coincidence will cut into growth, raise unemployment further, add to the costs of EMU before it starts. Monetary authorities have shown no disposition to accommodate. They have their own agenda: hold tight to the last moment, help shape the right attitude for the new Central Bank. The combination of overly tight monetary policy and determined budget cutting suggest a tough time ahead for Europe."[21]

The realization that EMU promises profound changes in the European lifestyle has forged an unlikely political alliance between left-wing Social Democrats and right-wing nationalists to defeat common money—at least, the hard EMU variety.

"As the 1997 deadline for deciding who will join EMU draws near, many Europeans are realizing that a single currency involves more than simply switching from marks or francs or gilders into Euro, the name chosen for the common currency," reports the *Wall Street Journal*. "By imposing strict budgetary, debt and inflation ceilings on member states, EMU would radically change Europe's way of life. It would force an overhaul of what Mr. Chirac (current President of France) calls 'the European social model'—a mixture of generous welfare spending, protective labor legislation and a strong government role as employer, shareholder, regulator and provider of 'public services' ranging from telecommunications to health and education. . . .

"All over Europe, the austerity policies that underpin the single currency are coming under fire. In Germany's biggest postwar demonstration, 350,000 people recently marched in Bonn to protest social spending cutbacks. In France, which endured three weeks of crippling strikes in December, unions are calling for walkouts this fall to protest public-sector job cuts. In Spain, unions are calling for a general strike against government plans to privatize an array of state companies. In Italy, union protests forced the government to soften its tough stand on public-sector wages."[22]

In Europe, it's EMU not free trade that threatend Europe's welfare state.

Should America Bully Its Standards onto Others?

"Would you buy a rug if you knew that it had been woven in India by 10-year-olds beaten if they didn't work fast enough?" "Would you wear a shirt if it had been sewn by a 9-year-old locked into a factory in Bangladesh until production quotas for the day had been met?" "Would you eat sardines if the cans had been filled by 12-year-old Filipino children sold into bonded servitude?"[23] These are questions Anna Quindlen posed to readers of her November 23, 1994 column in the *New York Times*.

Trade—or, more precisely, trade restrictions—has become the weapon of choice for U.S. human rights advocates who want to bludgeon poorer countries—India, Bangladesh, the Philippines are all examples—into accepting U.S. fair-labor standards for their own countries. "Child labor is the dirty little secret of foreign imports," writes Quindlen. "Senator Tom Harkin, who wants to outlaw U.S. imports of all products made by children under age 15, says the problem is that Americans don't know that some of what they buy, including toys for their own kids, has been manufactured by children working the kind of hours, under the kind of conditions, that many still associate with the darkest days of the Industrial Revolution."[24]

"Nearly half—about 45 percent—of all toys sold in the United States are produced for brand-name companies by contractors in China, Thailand and other countries in Asia," writes Bob Herbert, Miss Quindlen's former colleague on the op-ed page of the *New York Times*.[25] "The toy companies have embraced the Far East sweatshops for the same reason as other industries: There is an enormous supply of semi-slave laborers, including legions of poor and ignorant women and young girls, who will work for grotesquely low wages in disgusting and extremely dangerous conditions.

"U.S. executives keep the misery at a distance through the mechanism of contracts and subcontracts. They act as if they bear no responsibility for the exploitation of the men, women and children upon whom so much of their corporate profits rest.

"Most corporations will follow the trail of profits no matter how gruesome the human costs. Consumers are another matter. I believe there are very few American parents who would not be troubled by

the knowledge that a toy they were buying was produced by laborers—often children themselves—in a permanent state of degradation
and danger."[26]

"Mr. Harkin's bill to keep products made with child labor out of
the United States would probably be a violation of GATT," writes
Quindlen. "During various GATT negotiations, developing countries
successfully argued against child labor provisions, insisting that children have always worked in their cultures, that to try to interfere
with child labor is protectionist and punitive when a child may be
the only wage-earner in a desperately poor family. . . . If GATT passes,
an opportunity to end these children's servitude will have been
shunted aside for the alleged bonanza of free trade."[27]

Ms. Quindlen is not an economist and can be forgiven if she
doesn't fully appreciate the benefits of comparative advantage. And it
is true, of course, that child labor is an abomination to most Americans. But the former syndicated columnist really should recognize
that different cultures have different values, and that it is wrong and
ultimately counterproductive for the United States to threaten other
countries—particularly poorer ones—with financial penalties if they
do not adopt U.S. cultural standards. Ms. Quindlen and Senator
Harkin need to be reminded: bullying poorer and weaker countries is
as inconsistent with American values of fair play as is child labor.

Besides, the choices available to many really poor children in poor
countries is not between a lousy job (by U.S. standards) and a good job.
It is between a lousy job and no job. Lucy Martinez-Mont is an economics professor at Francisco Marroquin University in Guatemala
City. She wrote a response to Kathie Lee Gifford's crusade against
Central American sweatshops that use child labor to manufacture
clothing for export to the United States. "It is easy to understand,"
writes Professor Martinez-Mont in the *Wall Street Journal*, "why nice
people in rich countries are aghast at the working conditions in Central American factories. It is true that thousands of children work
nights, that workers are locked in until production quotas are fulfilled,
that wages are obscenely low, and that, in extreme cases, women and
children are beaten up by their supervisors. But it is also true that
there are no slaves in Central America. People choose to work in the
maquila shops of their own free will, because those are the best jobs
available to them. Given that unemployment compensation is
unheard of in Central America, a lousy job is better than no job at all.

"To those who live comfortable lives in the United States, it may be
hard to understand how anyone could become worse off if maquila
employment declined. But desperately poor countries can't afford to

forgo jobs in the name of better working conditions. That is one of the luxuries of development. . . . A visit to Central American slums, which lack even running water, or to Central American plantations, where 10-year-olds work long hours under the relentless sun, has helped many concerned foreigners grasp the true meaning of poverty. Depriving developing countries, even with the best of intentions, of capital and jobs needed to grow out of these centuries-old conditions of poverty will merely ensure the indefinite perpetuation of this misery."[28]

Though the intentions of "nice people" like Quindlen, Herbert, and Gifford to help children of poor countries are undoubtedly sincere, the motives of the U.S. trade-union movement in opposing child labor abroad is certainly open to question. U.S. trade unions want to protect noncompetitive U.S. apparel workers and manufacturers from foreign imports—not poor children in Guatemala, Honduras, and Mexico from unscrupulous bosses. The U.S. trade unions are using the poor children of Central America as an excuse to advance their own economic interests.

Indeed, as the Guatemalan economics professor points out, poor children in these countries would be made even poorer were the U.S. trade-union movement to succeed in its thinly disguised protectionist campaign against cheap foreign imports. What are the people of Central America to do if the export of one of the few goods in which they have a comparative advantage is blocked by U.S. protectionism? One thing is emigrate to the United States. The shutdown of sweatshops in Guatemala City will mean more sweatshops in New York City and other U.S. cities—and higher apparel prices to U.S. consumers as well. The way to help poor people abroad is to open our markets to them—not force them to adopt U.S. human-rights standards.

But perhaps the most forceful argument against the use of trade sanctions for human-rights purposes is practical rather than ethical—the sanctions are not likely to work. "Few countries," writes David Sanger in the *New York Times*, "are prepared to allow international trade inspectors to come to their factories and press questions like this: 'Excuse me, how old is that little girl who is gluing the leather soles of those shoes?' or 'Could you show us how you treat the chemicals coming out of this factory before you dump them in the river?' Or even: 'Why do you imprison workers who demand to make more than 50 cents an hour?'"[29]

Even the Clinton administration—after an unsuccessful attempt to force China to adopt U.S. human-rights policies to avoid U.S. trade restrictions—appears to have gotten the message that linking trade and human-rights concerns can be counterproductive. "If anything, the Clinton Administration has backed away from linking such domestic political issues to trade," writes Sanger. "The underlying message of its decision earlier this year to remove China's human rights record from the question of whether to renew its preferential trade status is that commerce is commerce, and connecting it to politics is just an invitation for America's competitors—Japan and the European Union—to move into markets while the United States stands on principle."

"Moreover," writes the *New York Times* reporter, "getting 124 countries as varied as Malaysia and Sweden to agree on common labor or environmental standards would be next to impossible. President Suharto of Indonesia made it clear to President Clinton last month that he was not interested in talking about why his country throws labor leaders in jail. Singapore's founder, Lee Kuan Yew, has forcefully argued that Western interference in 'Asian values,' including a national right to economic development that supersedes most individual rights."[30]

The Asian nations have made it clear they will not be bullied into adopting Western human rights standards. They may try to bribe Western leaders to delink trade from human rights. But these self-confident nations will not capitulate to foreign human rights ideas regardless of the commercial pressure placed on them by human rights activists like Oxfam, Christian Aid, and Unicef. These charities pose a distinct threat to Western interests, first, by encouraging Western protection against Asian exports on child labor grounds and, second, by souring long-term strategic relations between Asian and Western nations.

While the Clinton administration apparently has backed away from linking trade to social issues, it hasn't forsworn the threat of trade sanctions in purely commercial disputes. When in early 1995 negotiations stalled between China and the United States over alleged Chinese piracy of compact and laser discs, video games, films, books, and magazines, Mickey Kantor, the pugnacious former U.S. trade representative, announced punitive sanctions against 1.08 billion dollars of Chinese imports if no agreement was reached by a certain specified date. China was not slow to counter by threatening a mixture of sanctions and other penalties against U.S. business, including a freeze on negotiations involving carmakers seeking to establish joint ventures.

Even after it backed down in the dispute with China over human rights, the Clinton team apparently still didn't get the message that U.S. trade sanctions do not give this country sufficient leverage to change China's behavior. Perhaps the Clinton team felt that in its purely commercial dispute with China it had the U.S. business community on its side. "In a real war," writes Thomas Friedman of the *New York Times*, " you count tanks and soldiers. In a trade war, you count C.E.O.'s."[31] You also should count the ability of each side to sustain pain.

U.S. business leaders may indeed support President Clinton in his effort to secure U.S. intellectual property rights in China, but the U.S. is a democracy and China is an authoritarian society. This gives China an enormous advantage should U.S. push come to Chinese shove. In a trade war, consumers and producers on both sides are bound to suffer. But unlike U.S. leaders, China's authorities can safely ignore the anguish of Chinese consumers and producers. There are strict limits on dissent in China. Other things being equal, the internal pressure on democratic leaders to settle trade disputes is much greater than that imposed on autocratic ones.

But whichever country, China or the United States, has more leverage in trade disputes, there is a question as to whether it is proper for the U.S. government to impose trade sanctions on foreign nations like China that harbor pirates and counterfeiters of U.S. products. If Microsoft Corporation, for example, has its products stolen by Chinese counterfeiters, as it apparently does, the problem is essentially Microsoft's. The U.S. government has no proper role to play in this case. It certainly is wrong for the government to try to bail out Microsoft, and similarly situated companies, by imposing trade sanctions on China. For why should totally innocent American consumers of U.S.-sanctioned goods (consumers of textiles and clothing, for example) pay higher prices for these goods—and why should totally innocent U.S. companies and their workers be deprived of jobs and profits from doing business in China, as they surely will be when China responds to the U.S. sanctions by imposing retaliatory sanctions of their own on U.S. firms—so that Microsoft stockholders can have greater profits? Moreover, while the costs of the trade sanctions to the many are certain, the benefit of the sanctions to the few are less certain. There is no guarantee the sanctions will have their desired result. Imposing trade sanctions on China can lead to a permanently ruptured trade relation between the two countries. The best thing for the U.S. government to do in face of Chinese piracy is to do nothing!

Not only human-rights but animal-rights activists are attempting to use trade as leverage to impose their values on foreign countries. "British animal rights protesters claimed victory on Friday when

Swansea airport dropped plans to take cargoes of livestock," reports the *Financial Times*. "Earlier this month, protesters also blocked shipments of live lambs and calves from the West Sussex port of Shoreham. Now the demonstrators are targeting other British ports and airports which accept live cargoes. . . . The protester's objective is a ban on the 200 million pound-sterling annual UK trade in selling livestock to continental Europe."[32] Why? Because the protesters view continental Europe's treatment of livestock to be inhumane.

The protesters are right—Continental Europe does mistreat livestock. But, as the editors of the *Financial Times* argue, the United Kingdom has neither the means nor the right to impose their values on other countries. "Although the UK has banned putting calves in crates since 1990," writes the editors, "it does not have the means to impose that stance on other countries. Under current laws, it cannot prevent foreign purchasers of British animals treating those animals in whatever manner they choose. Nor, under existing European trade laws, can it ban exports because of distaste about their eventual fate. Moreover, the UK does not have a clear moral right to impose its views on animals on other countries."[33]

Free intra-union trade—the *sine qua non* of the European Union—would be little more than a dream if each country protested with trade restrictions what they found objectionable in other member countries. "If [animal rights] protesters want to advance their cause," write the *Financial Times* editors, "the right route is to urge MPs and Euro MPs to muster support among European Union countries for a change in rules. . . . If protesters can change European law through legitimate representation, that is all to the good."[34]

A final point. While protestors who seek to link the conduct of international trade to the human-rights, workers-rights, and animal-rights policies of partner countries are undoubtedly sincere, the movement itself is being exploited by protectionists, who care little for these causes, but know a good cover for protectionism when they see one. France, for example, recently announced its intention to press its European Union partners to support a campaign in the World Trade Organization and other bodies to link labor standards with trade policy. "Many countries see the initiative as thinly veiled protectionism," reports the *Financial Times*.[35] U.K. employment secretary Michael Portillo said "social clauses would raise costs in poorer countries and 'would deny them market access, condemning the world's poor to perpetual poverty.' . . . The initiative is part of a wider campaign by the French government to develop what it calls 'an authentic European social model.' This would include provisions for participation by employers' and workers' representatives in drafting EU social legislation, closer EU co-operation on the link between work organization and an ageing labor force and a five-year European programme for vocational training."[36]

Trading nations of the world beware: the proposed "European Social model" is really a "European protectionist model" clothed in welfare-state platitudes.

The Subsidy Spillover

One mechanism by which the welfare state encourages protection is by slowing economic growth and stifling job creation. Another is by subsidizing certain domestic activities of, and geographic areas in, the welfare state which "spill over" onto its exports. A regional grant to bolster the fortunes of a depressed area is a typical welfare-state egalitarian policy. Its motive is protection of a designated geographic region, but the fact that companies resident in the favored area may export abroad gives foreign competitors an excuse to claim backdoor export subsidization and demand their government take "compensatory measures." Such measures often take the form of tariffs and other trade restricting interventions.

Industrial subsidies are another favorite form of welfare-state intervention which can lead to restrictions on trade between countries. "The United States charges that Canadian hog farmers get unfair government subsidies, hurting U.S. hog farmers but enabling American consumers to buy cheaper pork chops and bacon," reports the *New York Times*. "So the Commerce Department retaliates by slapping higher duties on Canadian pork. Not to be outdone, Canada alleges unfair American subsidies to American corn growers and hits imports of American corn. Both Canada and the United States set higher tariffs on each other's steel, each saying the other prices unfairly. On and on it goes—hogs, corn, steel, wheat, lumber, you name it. The countries with the biggest two-way trading relationship are almost constantly kicking each others shins over unfair trade."[37]

What should be done to limit future U.S.-Canadian trade imbroglios? The answer is clear: reduce the subsidies and the trade conflicts are reduced *para passu*.

But reducing industrial and regional subsidies in the welfare state is no easy matter. Subsidies serve a variety of purposes critical to the welfare state. One is to enforce welfare-state objectives of preventing labor movements within the domestic economy. In a competitive economy, labor mobility is essential to promoting efficiency in the domestic allocation of resources. Today's welfare state, however, frowns on labor mobility because it is alleged to damage the nation's social fabric.

Subsidies to encourage workers to stay put are part of a more generalized "worker's rights" movement in the welfare state. Citizens of the modern welfare state believe they have a right not only to free speech, press and assembly, but to a job, in the industry of their choice, at the geographic location of their choice, and at an income that permits *politically determined* minimum consumption standards. Economic and political rights go hand in hand in the welfare state. The subsidy is a key instrument in securing workers their so-called "economic rights."

Spillover problems in the welfare state are not limited to subsidies spilling over onto exports. Social services spill over onto migrant workers in welfare states, which lead to pressures to limit the migration of foreign workers to countries that need their services.

Public opinion in the welfare state often is hostile to offering "free" medical, educational, and other social services to migrants. It also is hostile to migrants benefiting from domestic affirmative action programs. This is particularly true when the migrants are in the country of public largesse illegally.

Rather than lead to the demand that the welfare state and affirmative action be scaled back, however, more often than not the demand is made that labor migration be restricted. What the public does not appear to be sufficiently aware of is that foreign workers— even illegals—often do pay taxes so that the social services they receive are not free. Moreover, migrants—legal and illegal—create *private* income and wealth in this country, which in turn create tax revenues for city, state, and federal governments. The social services migrants absorb are—at least in part—paid for by these tax revenues (as well as by the direct taxes migrants pay). Finally, migrants can be paying for the social services they use in this country by accepting a lower wage in the United States than is generally available on competitive world markets. Economic analysis tells us that so long as the real income from the *sum* of the U.S. wage plus the social services spillovers is greater than the world wage alone, migrants can be expected to bid down the U.S. wage *below* what would be obtainable elsewhere. Thus if the wage for a certain type of labor is six dollars an hour on world labor markets, migrants might be willing to work in the United States for five dollars an hour so that they can take advantage of U.S. social services. This creates even more private income and wealth in the United States than if the migrant were just to receive the competitive world wage here.

The preferred response to the problem of social service spillovers to migrants in the welfare state is to limit the welfare state, not the migrants. Yet demagogic politicians scapegoat legal and illegal migrants as if they were worthless deadbeats who take from the community but give nothing in return. Governor Pete Wilson of California, for example, made Proposition 187—which denies state social services, including education, to illegal migrants and their children—a centerpiece of his reelection campaign in 1994. Burdened by a deep recession and a bloated welfare state, Californians let their nativism get the best of their judgement and passed Proposition 187 by a wide margin (they also reelected Governor Wilson).

Proposition 187 turned out to be good politics for Wilson but bad public policy for California. Attacking the illegal migrants, and not the welfare state, is equivalent to attacking the symptoms of a disease rather than its causes. *Wall Street Journal* columnist Paul Gigot thinks "Mr. Wilson is lucky he isn't pressed about who really is responsible for immigration costs. Illegal immigration is much less a burden in Texas, which sustains a much less generous welfare state. One 1985 study found that 85 percent of all refugees in California were on welfare within three years. But in Texas fewer than 20 percent were. Of course it's easier to campaign against illegal immigrants, who don't vote, than against welfare lobbies and teachers unions, which surely do."[38]

Gigot's conclusion is supported by the experience of Ron Unz, a Silicon Valley businessman who challenged Pete Wilson in the 1993 Republican gublinatorial primary. Here is what Unz has to say about his race against Wilson:

> In December 1993, while considering a primary challenge to Governor Pete Wilson of California, I commissioned an extremely detailed survey of 1,200 Republican primary voters, with one of the main sections being an analysis of their views on the crucial issue of immigration.
>
> At first glance, the results seemed to confirm the conventional wisdom on illegal immigration, with the respondents rating "stopping illegal immigration at the border" at 4.3 in importance (on a scale of 1–5), second only to crime control (4.5), and slightly ahead of job creation and tax limitation. But when voters were then asked the reasons behind their immigration concerns (in two parallel subsamples of 600 each, dealing with illegal and legal immigrants

respectively), neither legal nor legal immigrants were viewed as taking jobs away from other Californians, as committing much crime,
or as generally turning California into a "Third World" state. The
only issues that raised significant concerns were the financial drain
of illegal immigrants on welfare (4.1), fears that legal and illegal
immigrants weren't learning English in the schools (3.2 combined),
and anger that legal and illegal immigrants and their children would
benefit unfairly from affirmative action (3.3 combined).

Next, respondents were informed that some studies showed
that most illegal/legal immigrants were paying taxes, obeying laws,
trying to learn English, and weren't on welfare; by better than 2–1
the response was that under such circumstances, immigration was
not a serious problem in California. Following this, the respondents
indicated by a margin of nearly 4–1 that they agreed that immigration were being unfairly blamed by politicians for problems like
crime and welfare, which were more connected with the native-
born urban, underclass than with legal and illegal immigrants.

Finally, a subsample of 600 was informed that a hypothetical
candidate believed that immigrants—both legal and illegal—were
being scapegoated by politicians, and that if welfare benefits were
cut and bilingual education and affirmative action stopped, then
immigration would again become an actual plus for California. A
majority of the subsample agreed, and more significantly, the voters
of this subsample were willing to support the hypothetical candidate on a sample ballot just as strongly as were the other 600 subsample: A pro-immigration stance had incurred no political cost. All
of this data indicate that the immigration issue is largely proxy for
concerns about welfare, affirmative action, bilingual education, and
multiculturalism, and is much broader than it is deep.

The result of my actual gubernatorial primary race supports
this conclusion. Despite my complete lack of name recognition or
political experience, my being outspent nearly four to one by Governor Wilson, and my public opposition to immigrant bashing, in
just eight weeks of campaigning I raised support from 8 percent to
34 percent by election day, including nearly half of all Republican
voters age 50 and under."[39]

A final and related point: While the welfare-cutting Republicans
in the U.S. Congress seem to be on the right track to moderate illegal
immigration by moderating welfare, certain Republicans (U.S.
Senator Alan Simpson and U.S. Representative Lamar Smith) have
taken a wrong turn on the illegal migrant problem. Instead of cutting
the welfare state, Simpson and Smith argue for a new federal computer system to approve every American new hire. "Each year,"
writes Paul Gigot,[40] "there are about 65 million job hires in the U.S.

And for every one, an employer would have to deal what Republican Steve Chabot of Ohio calls a '1–800-Big-Brother' number to certify an employee's citizenship."

If this is not bad enough, the computer system is seen by its advocates as a prelude to the even more Draconian measure—the national ID card. "Messrs. Simpson and Smith swear no surly intention," continues Gigot. "But Florida Rep. Bill McCollum, whose charm is his lack of subtlety, gave the game away at a hearing last week. Even computer verification won't work he said, 'unless we wind up with an identification system that is more tamperproof than' today's Social Security card. Such as? 'There will be a picture, a hardened card a hologram. Perhaps there will be a biometric identifier,' Mr. McCollum said, 'which would mean a fingerprint or retina scan.'"

Gigot concludes, "If Republicans want to eliminate one immigrant magnet, they can always reduce welfare. If its cultural assimilation they seek, then bar bilingual education. But on the list of America's great problems, people who *want* to work, even at the minimum wage, aren't at the top."[40]

5

No Cheers
for Foreign Aid

Income transfer is the *sine qua non* of the modern welfare state. To secure for itself a preeminent role in the distribution of the nation's production of goods and services, the government uses its substantial tax, spending, subsidization, and administrative powers to take from Citizen A to give to Citizen B. Not that the welfare state is the "Robin Hood" state, though that is what its proponents would like us to believe. For at the same time that government takes from Citizen A to give to B, it also takes from Citizen B to give to A. Each citizen, in other words, has debits and credits in its account with government, and whether one comes out with a *net* credit or debit balance in the end depends on a host of factors and not simply how much money one earns in private life.

The modern welfare state may have started with the "safety net" concept, but it has evolved into something infinitely more complex and dangerous—the socialization of income and wealth distribution.

Foreign aid is the extension of welfare-state-style income transfer from the domestic to the international level. Income is transferred, not from Citizen A to Citizen B, but from the *government* of Country A to the *government* of Country B. The common perception is that foreign aid is a means by which rich donor countries help poor people in foreign lands. The reality is something much different.

Foreign Aid's Dirty Little Secret

Poor people in foreign lands see very few foreign aid dollars donor countries spend on their behalf. Official aid—and sometimes even private aid—must go through recipient governments. And these governments use the aid for their own purposes, which can be—and often are—at variance with the welfare of the general populace. Western countries, for example, gave the Ethiopian government millions of dollars worth of food for hunger relief during the '80s civil war. But the government used the food, not to feed the innocent victims of the war, as donor countries intended, but to feed their victimizers, the Ethiopian army.

In Bangladesh—one of the world's poorest countries—Western food aid also was intended for the very poor. But it too never reached its destination. Instead, the government used the food to prop up its political support among Bangladesh's influential middle class. "It comes as a surprise to a layman, but not at all to the experts," writes Barry Newman in the *Wall Street Journal*, "that food aid arriving in Bangladesh and many other places isn't used to feed the poor. *Governments typically sell the food on local markets and use the proceeds however they choose*. Here, the government chooses to sell the food in cut-rate ration shops to members of the middle class."[1]

The United States sent its army into Somalia in a direct attempt to get its food aid to Somalia's poor. But this too didn't work. Warring factions were responsible for Somalia's hunger and devastation, and when the United States directly intervened—like it or not—we too became a part of the civil strife. When enough American soldiers were sent home in body bags, U.S. ardor to help Somalia's poor cooled and the U.S. troops withdrew.

Foreign aid's dirty little secret is that U.S. foreign-aid dollars often wind up in numbered Swiss bank accounts and palatial estates of third world tyrants—not in the pockets of the poor.

Foreign Aid and Policy Mistakes

That the poor receive little of the foreign aid intended for them is but one of the little-known facts about foreign aid. Equally important is that foreign aid can—and often does—prolong and exacerbate the poverty its purpose is to alleviate. Poor countries are not poor because some higher power ordains it, but for the more mundane reason that their governments follow bad economic policies—e.g., runaway public spending, protectionism, price controls, and excessive money creation. By temporarily moderating the symptoms of policy mistakes, foreign aid perpetuates the mistakes and thus the poverty that results from them.

"By ameliorating the symptoms of economic collapse," write Doug Bandow and Ian Vasquez, "multilateral aid is more likely to postpone the adoption of necessary reforms. Governments that receive foreign assistance find it easier to avoid making the politically difficult decisions typically required by economic restructuring. Suspending or reducing aid, on the other hand, is far more effective at inducing governments to implement the liberalization necessary for sustainable growth."[2]

A clear example of this is Castro in Cuba. For decades Cuba was on the dole from the Soviet Union. Among other things, this aid allowed the Cubans to follow socialist economic policies which literally ruined their economy. Without the aid, Castro would have been forced to be less ideological and more cognizant of market forces. This is clear now that the Soviet aid has been shut down. Though Castro resists, his government nonetheless is making market reforms—and many more will come.

Vietnam is another example of a country where the cutoff of Soviet aid has liberated the economy. Bandow and Vasquez write: "Vietnam, which until recently was excluded from receiving World Bank and IMF loans, reacted to the cutoff of massive Soviet aid by implementing economic reforms that led to a 'vigorously emerging private sector' and an annual economic growth rate of 3 percent in 1991. New loans from the World Bank and IMF, however, may delay the reform process." An editorial in the *Far Eastern Economic Review* noted that Vietnam might be better off alone.

> Vietnam has done a remarkable job restoring its economy with its doi moi, or renovation policy.... And its isolation from the well-intentioned multilateral lending agencies has been another blessing in disguise. Look at the Philippines, a prime target of these loans, and now saddled with nearly $29 billion in debt and nothing to show for it. Contrast this with the rapid prosperity of say, Hong Kong, left happily unperturbed by the attentions of these lenders. To be sure, the multilaterals mean well and in recent years have urged more open markets.... [But] experience suggests that their usual terms of credit and in-built bias toward a top-down approach to development are no substitute for market discipline."[3]

Taiwan is another country where the cutoff of foreign aid provided the springboard for unparalleled economic growth. The donor in the case of Taiwan was the United States, not the Soviet Union. The United States gave Taiwan substantial economic assistance until the mid-1960s. This aid was used in part to support Taiwan's chronically weak currency, and finance its perpetual balance of payments deficits. The reason for the payments deficits and weak currency was the country's hostility to foreign investment, and protectionist import-substitution policies.

When the United States finally did shut off the aid spigot, Taiwan was compelled to renounce protectionism and liberalize its capital import policies. Otherwise, its lack of foreign exchange would have dramatically reduced living standards in the island nation. In effect, the U.S. aid had subsidized and sustained bad economic policies in Taiwan. When the aid was terminated, so were the bad policies.

What happened to Taiwan in the 1960s is extremely relevant to what happened to Mexico thirty years later in the 1990s. Mexico got itself into serious trouble because it used imported savings to finance bloated living standards (see Chapter One). Capital inflow, attracted by high short-term interest rates and the promise of a fixed peso, allowed the Mexicans to run a large trade deficit and consume above their means for some time. Eventually, Mexican profligate spending came to an abrupt end when skepticism concerning the Zedillo government's continued ability to fix the peso's exchange rate caused international investors to run for the nearest exit. The peso crashed, capital was withdrawn from Mexican markets, and the previously unthinkable possibility of exchange controls suddenly became thinkable as Mexican foreign-exchange reserves dwindled to dangerously low levels.

In these circumstances, the international community—namely, the United States, the International Monetary Fund, and several G-7 countries—panicked and gave Mexico a fifty billion dollar loan to support the peso and rollover part of its substantial debt. Was the loan wise? Supporters of the bailout, such as U.S. Fed Chairman Alan Greenspan and I.M.F. head Michel Camdessus, warned of "systemic crisis" and a "true world catastrophe" if the loan was not made. M.I.T. economist Rudi Dornbusch concurred. "The lender of last resort," writes Dornbusch, "comes in not to reward a poorly managed debtor but to avoid the spill over effects of a credit system connected by confidence or contagion. A Mexican default and collapse will spill over to our own economy and bring down other economies, most immediately Argentina. The incidence is not primarily on the creditors who may well deserve the lesson and on Mexicans but goes far beyond. With plenty of fragility in Latin America, once there is a crack in the system bank run mentality takes over. Very few institutions and countries can stand up to that. We also owe some loyalty to our product: having preached open, modern and deregulated economies a failure to back up our model risks giving the advantage to the retrograde camp: Cardenas, Mexico's unreconstructed left wing leader is already on the march."[4]

The distinguished voices of Mssrs. Greenspan, Camdessus, and Dornbusch, in this case at least, are the voices of expediency. For sound economic policy, one must turn to the editorial pages of the *Financial Times*. "What is certain", write the *Financial Times* editors, "is that action to avert an alleged systemic crisis is bound to encourage the kind of behaviour that will lead to the next one. Investors will, for example, now be encouraged to advance short-term funds in the belief that industrial countries will take care of any liquidity problems. This is a sure way of making the financial system more fragile under the guise of making it safer." Economists call this the "moral hazard" problem.

"The fundamental issue," continue the *Financial Times* editors, "is what this huge rescue signifies. Mr. Camdessus argues that the intervention had been required to underpin the credibility of the market-oriented approach to development. What it does is undermine it. It does so by substituting official for private capital, by offering implicit insurance to private capital flows, by making unsound private finance more probable and, most important, by indicating a lack of confidence in the self-correcting capacity of financial markets. If this is what the authorities really believe, how can they continue to justify reliance on private capital flows to developing countries at all?"[5]

Even Fed chairman Greenspan recognizes what he himself has called the "perverse incentive effects" of the Mexican bailout. By neutralizing the costs of past policy errors in Mexico, we encourage future ones. The conditionality the U.S. Treasury imposed on U.S. loans to Mexico probably will do little good. The Mexicans agreed to conditionality because (1) they had no choice and (2) they feel they can renegotiate new terms later on if need be. When push comes to shove, the Mexicans probably believe the United States will renegotiate for the same reasons it offered the loans in the first place—to starve off a full-blown Mexican financial crisis. Thus, by making Mexico's problems U.S. problems, the U.S. loses whatever leverage it may have had in negotiating with our neighbors to the South.

The Foreign Aid Shortfall

An important policy point emerges from the foregoing analyses: the net gain to recipient countries from foreign aid will be less than the value of the transferred resources themselves, because foreign aid perpetuates major policy mistakes that destroy resources in the recipient country. The value of these destroyed resources must be subtracted from the value of the foreign aid to obtain the net gain from aid, which raises the possibility that foreign aid actually can have a negative net value added to the *recipient* country as well as the donor. If the value of the resources destroyed by policy mistakes directly (and indirectly) attributable to foreign aid are greater than the value of the transferred aid, both donor and recipient countries lose.

Macroeconomic policy errors are not the only negative, offsetting consequence of foreign aid. The purpose of food aid, for example, is to increase the quantity of food available to feed poor people. Assuming for the moment the donated food actually can get through to the poor people for whom it is intended—an unrealistic assumption but a useful one for the purpose at hand—it easily can be demonstrated that the gain, in terms of food available for domestic consumption, must be less than the transferred food itself. This is because food aid lowers food prices in recipient countries, which causes domestic farmers to reduce their output of food.

Moreover, the reduction in food prices redistributes income from local producers to local consumers. Since it is the local producers who must invest in the land, food production also can be expected to decline because of land neglect. Less profits from the land mean less funds available for investment in the land. The reduction in domestic production of food—from both price and income-transfer effects— must be subtracted from the food aid to ascertain the net gain, if any, from foreign assistance.

The experience of Colombia is interesting in this regard. Dudley and Sandilands point out that between 1953 and 1971, wheat imported into Colombia under food aid rose from 50 to 90 percent of total wheat consumption.[6] During that same period, the price for wheat declined by one-half, and wheat production in Colombia declined to one-third its original level. The conventional interpretation—that food aid increased because of declining food production— is less convincing than the alternative—that wheat production declined because of increasing food aid. The logic of the supply curve, after all, is that output falls when price falls, not the reverse.

Aid Versus Trade

The argument that foreign aid is good for recipient countries depends on its *net* value added being positive—and this assumes all elements of cost are included in the calculus. But in properly defining cost, it often is overlooked that foreign aid can be—and usually is—a substitute for some other policy measure that would take place in the absence of aid—such as improved access to the markets of donor countries.

When the Berlin Wall came down, for example, the West Europeans gave the Easterners substantial amounts of aid, not solely for humanitarian reasons, but also because they wanted Easterners to remain in Eastern Europe and were not willing to give Eastern exports improved access to their markets. "The new democracies of Eastern Europe complain bitterly that the EC is hampering their path to post-Communist prosperity by blocking the entry of many of their products" write Peter Gumbel and Charles Goldsmith in the *Wall Street Journal*.[7] Western Europe, however, has turned a deaf ear to these complaints: "We give them plenty of aid," Westerners argue, "what are they complaining about?"

The answer to this query is clear. What they are complaining about is that poorer countries lose more from developed countries' protectionism than they gain from their aid. J. Michael Finger of the World Bank calculates that "developed countries' import restrictions reduce developing countries' national income by about twice as much as developing countries receive in aid."[8] Moreover, foreign aid builds up the resources of government at a time when the need is to build up the private sector. "It is indeed a tragedy," writes Melanie Tammen of the CATO Institute, "that the United States and its European allies are showering the new democracies of Eastern Europe with the same programs of subsidized, government-to-government loans that have financed big government throughout the developing world while maintaining substantial barriers to key Eastern European exports in areas as diverse as agriculture and textiles."[9]

The United States and Western Europe are supposed to be promoting a market- oriented approach to development in the former Soviet satellites. They need to show it by liberalizing their import restrictions and reducing their economic aid.

Aid Grows the Welfare State

Aid is both a consequence of the welfare state in donor countries and a cause of the welfare state in recipient countries. Israel is a well-known case where foreign aid has created an elaborate welfare state. "The economy of Israel is unusually dependent on foreign grants, loans and charity," writes Alvin Rabushka.[10] "Such aid has allowed the European socialists who founded the country, and their ideological successors, to build economic institutions—strong trade unions, massive regulations and big government—that are inappropriate to today's competitive world." The aid and consequent welfare state also explains why Israel is bereft of inward foreign private investment. "Know how to make a small fortune in Israel?," goes the old joke. "Bring in a large fortune!" Its a good thing Israelis have a sense of humor.

Not all foreign aid consists in explicit intergovernmental budgetary transfers. Indeed the most dramatic example of U.S. foreign aid financing a foreign welfare state is NATO, the North Atlantic Treaty Organization. When the United States paid for European defense after World War II, the resources Europe would have put into its own defense were freed to finance Europe's welfare state. How could the Europeans possibly have paid for the most expensive welfare state known to man if they, rather than American taxpayers, had to pay for the U.S. troops in Germany, the nuclear missiles located throughout Europe . . . , and so on?

NATO also created European defense weakness—and a defense dependency—that was good neither for Europe nor for the United States. Dependency is a classic symptom of aid. When a poor country receives food aid, for example, domestic food production falls in the recipient country, and its dependence on the donor country for food increases. Similarly, when Europe underinvests in its own defense because of defense free-riding on Uncle Sam, its dependence on the United States for defense support increases *para passu*.

Sometimes, of course, the not-so-hidden purpose of aid is precisely to create dependencies which are expected to give donor countries increased leverage over the policies of their beneficiaries. The Europeans, however, have been very comfortable with NATO, calculating—correctly, I believe—that their superior diplomatic skills would protect them from the expected disadvantages defense dependency otherwise would impose upon them vis à vis their benefactors. What better proof can there be of this than that U.S. support for NATO continues despite both the collapse of the common enemy and NATO's proven inability to deal with regional crises such as Bosnia?

Aid and National Security in the Post–Cold War Era

The "Dane-geld"

It is always a temptation to an armed and agile nation,
    To call upon a neighbour and to say:
"We invaded you last night—we are quite prepared to fight,
    Unless you pay us cash to go away."
        And that is called asking for Dane-geld,
        And the people who ask it explain
        That you've only to pay 'em the Dane-geld
        And then you'll get rid of the Dane!

It is always a temptation to a rich and lazy nation,
    To puff and look important and to say:
"Though we know we should defeat you, we have not the
        time to meet you,
We will therefore pay you cash to go away."
        And that is called paying the Dane-geld;
        But we've proved it again and again,
        That if once you have paid him the Dane-geld
        You never get rid of the Dane.

It is wrong to put temptation in the path of any nation,
    For fear they should succumb and go astray,
So when you are requested to pay up or be molested,
        You will find it better policy to say:
        "We never pay anyone Dane-geld,
        No matter how trifling the cost,
        For the end of that game is oppression and shame,
        And the nation that plays it is lost!"

                                        —Rudyard Kipling

Nothing beats national security as a justification of, and ratio-
nalization for, foreign aid. Before the collapse of communism, the
Right justified foreign aid because of the need to fight the spread of
communism in poor countries. In the post–Cold War era, it is the Left
who argues for foreign aid on national security grounds—allegedly to
fight the resurrection of communism and fascism in the former
Soviet Union.

An example *par excellence* of the latter is a 1994 Congressional
Budget Office study entitled "Enhancing U.S. Security Through Foreign Aid." "The United States should consider increased funding for

foreign assistance programs that can help meet national security goals," argues the CBO study. "Certain types of foreign aid—including monies for U.N. peacekeeping operations, international arms control efforts, and aid to the former Soviet republics—may in some cases be more effective than military weapons in dealing with problems such as arms proliferation and territorial disputes. Selected types of development assistance may help greatly in stemming the rapid population growth and economic deprivation that, especially over a period of years, can provide a breeding ground for extremist groups that cause political instability and violence—or that make it more difficult for governments to take politically difficult yet responsible steps in pursuit of peace."[11]

To justify its foreign-aid recommendations, the CBO study refers to the alleged success of the Marshall Plan and Pacific Basin countries. "Relying more on foreign aid to enhance national security," it claims, "would parallel the decision that followed victory in an earlier and quite different geopolitical conflict. In the late 1940s, the United States initiated the Marshall Plan, which helped rebuild the economies of Western Europe after World War II. In the first postwar decade, it also began large aid programs for several developing countries of Asia that became strong military and political allies."[12]

While these foreign-aid advocates have turned the foreign-aid experience and lesson from the Pacific Basin countries on its head, the Marshall Plan may be the one indisputable case where foreign aid actually did recipients some good. But just because a single plan worked, in a single circumstance, at a particular point of time, does not give it general applicability and relevance. Two leading international economists—the late Gottfried Haberler of Harvard University and Lord Bauer of The London School of Economics—argue that the success of the Marshall Plan was a unique occurrence not likely to be duplicated in today's poor countries.

"It is one thing to assist a war-ravished industrial country put its economy back on its feet," writes Haberler, "and it is an entirely different thing to help a less-developed, backward country change its way of life and modernize its economy."[13] Lord Bauer notes that "the success of the Marshall Plan in the early post-war years is frequently invoked in support of wealth transfer to the Third World. This analogy is altogether misleading. The damaged economies of Western Europe had to be revived, not developed. As was evident from pre-war experience, the personal, social, and political factors congenial to economic achievement were present."[14]

Clearly, the present situation of the former Soviet Union republics is closer to the "less-developed, backward country that has to change its way of life and modernize its economy" than the "war-ravished industrial country that has to put its economy back on its feet."

Notwithstanding this fact, the authors of the CBO study use national security to argue for the expenditure of billions of dollars of U.S. aid to Russia and the newly independent states of the former Soviet Union. "Some policymakers maintain that the Western world should provide what amounts to a financial cushion to help pensioners, the unemployed and other individuals particularly hurt by the high inflation and economic restructuring now occurring in the states of the former Soviet Union," argues the CBO study. "Other advocates of aid point to the need for effective arms control activities, such as a major effort to improve the control of military sensitive exports leaving the territories of the newly independent states. Still others propose giving more aid to Ukraine—even before it gives up its nuclear weapons—as a way to reassure that country about its sovereignty and induce it to support policies consistent with the national security interests of the United States. . . . Costs might be up to $10 billion a year for several years. The United States' contribution to such an effort, given its special security interest—shared also by Europe and Japan—in ensuring a successful reform process in the countries that make up the Soviet Union, might be about $3 billion a year."[15]

Anti-military types in this country have a serious national security problem. They want dramatic cutbacks in the U.S. military budget, and to make up for the resultant national security gap or shortfall, propose economic aid on the dubious grounds that economic aid and military expenditure are substitutes for one another from the national security point of view. But economic aid to the former Soviet Union can be expected to be as ineffectual in promoting U.S. security interests as the billions of dollars the U.S. misspent on a variety of Third World dictators who, during the Cold War period, became rich simply by proclaiming anti-communism and/or threatening to "switch sides" were sufficient U.S. handouts not forthcoming.

Does any serious person really believe, for example, that the billions the United States lavished on Ferdinand Marcos in the Philippines or the Contras in Nicaragua, over the years hastened the collapse of the Soviet Union by even a day?

Were the U.S. anti-military types to get their way and economic aid dispensed to Russia on a grand scale, those who would get rich this

time around would be power elites in the former Soviet republics—
not the pensioners, the unemployed, and the poor. Money would flow
from the American taxpayer to the U.S. Government, from the U.S.
Government to the governments of the former Soviet republics, and
from the governments of the former Soviet republics to numbered
Swiss bank accounts. How this redistribution of wealth would add to
U.S. national security is a big mystery.

Even in the most unlikely circumstance that U.S. economic aid
would get through to the intended recipients—and, I repeat, in the
former Soviet republics there need be little worry on that score—it is
the victory of socialist fallacy over the history of capitalistic states to
suggest that the establishment of a social-welfare safety net constitutes either a necessary or sufficient condition for capitalism to take
hold. For history is unambiguous that the social safety net, when it
has come, has always come after—not before—capitalism has made
society rich enough to believe it could afford the safety net in the first
place. In Northern Europe, for example, capitalism came first and the
social safety net after. The same is true in the United States and the
Pacific Basin region.

The truth of the matter is that what the U.S. anti-military types
really want is to replace the present exploitative governments in the
former Soviet republics with social-welfare governments. Then, they
tell us, the market reforms will go through, as if the principal obstacle to reform in the former Soviet republics are the pensioners, unemployed, and the poor. The real reason reforms don't go through is that
powerful vested interests in the former Soviet republics don't want
them to go through—either because they don't believe in a market
economy, or because their own pocketbooks would be adversely
affected by reform, or they have made a calculation that the longer
they delay the reforms, the more the West will pay for them in terms
of economic aid. The last mentioned is an inescapable result of the
perception in the former Soviet republics that Western leaders want
market reforms more than they do.

Does, then, Western aid help, or hurt, the reform process? No less
of an authority than the former Russian finance minister, Boris Fyodorov, argues aid hurts rather than helps. "I believe that in 1993, Russia's relations with the West were developing in the right direction,"
writes Fyodorov. "For me, it was not so much money as moral support that mattered. That is why when we saw, last August, that our
targets had not been achieved, I was the first to alert the International
Monetary Fund and our Government—though it would have been
easy to cook the figures and get the money. We decided not to lie to

ourselves and to the world.

"But now that the IMF has extended this loan, on the ground that it will be politically beneficial to the West, I say: Lock up the advisors who give such counsel and throw away the key.

"The sooner the IMF's money is handed over, the sooner we will see a change in policy—in the wrong direction. I recall how after each new loan, former President Mikhail S. Gorbachev would lose interest in any kind of economic reform.

"The $1.5 billion is immaterial to Russia, given the scale of its problems, and will be eaten up in a matter of minutes. Its importance is that it will be taken as a seal of approval on 'corrections' that have been made to Russia's economic policy.

"This is now a purely political matter. The stakes are high. *The idea of those in power is to abandon Western-type economic policies with Western approval.*"[16]

Boris Fyodorov's comments on the effect IMF aid is likely to have on the reform process in Russia should give us all pause for thought. It is one thing when a well-known critic like Peter Bauer or myself thrashes the IMF. It is quite another when an IMF aid *recipient* blasts the fund on similar grounds, that aid blocks needed reforms.

Nowhere is the naivete of aid advocates more evident than in their proposal for Western aid to finance an increase in the salaries of customs officials in the newly independent states, so that the officials would be less inclined to accept bribes to allow the export of dangerous technologies and weapons. "If customs officers are not receiving training or adequate salaries," argues the CBO study, "the United States may choose to improve their compensation levels and thus—it is hoped—reduce their temptation to permit the unauthorized export of weapons or weapons-related technologies. Depending on the scale of the effort, such a program to enhance export controls might cost the United States $200 million a year."[17]

Far better that the 200 million dollars be spent on America's poor than on some hair-brained foreign-aid scheme certain to fail! Can corrupt customs officials really be expected to forgo bribes simply because their salaries are increased? Of course not—they simply will take the increased salary plus the bribes! And if a deal could be made conditional upon forgoing bribes, how could we verify that bribing was not in fact continuing after the money was paid? The answer is we couldn't.

Implicit in this proposal is the assumption that corruption, like all bad things, comes from poverty, and therefore can be cured by government income transfer. In the case of corrupt customs officials, what income transfer, in fact, will do is *increase* the export of dangerous materials, so as to encourage Western countries to send even more foreign aid to the corrupt officials. Soviet customs officials, after all, cannot be expected to be as naive as aid advocates.

To spread disinformation that they are tough-minded, aid advocates argue that some of the aid they propose be made conditional upon the recipients making economic reforms. But while useful as political spin and propaganda to aid advocates, conditionality, in practice, seldom works. During the Cold War period, conditionality was not effective because the U.S. was in competition with the Soviet Union. The recipient countries knew and exploited this fact. As I wrote elsewhere: "So long as the Third World country knows the United States is using economic aid to compete with the Soviet Union, 'conditionality' will not be effective. The Third World country simply will take the aid and promise to make the reforms at some future date; then it breaks its promise, claiming severe domestic opposition to the reforms. When the United States counters by threatening an aid cutoff, the aid recipient responds with a threat of its own: 'If you cut the aid, we will go for help to the Soviets or to one of its proxy nations.' Finally, we decide the aid must be continued for national security reasons."[18]

Judging by the way the Clinton administration has thrown its weight behind Boris Yeltsin in Russia, a similar aid dynamic appears to be shaping up in the post–Cold War period. The U.S. gives Yeltsin conditional aid and he makes many promises. When the promises are not kept, the U.S. threatens to withdraw the aid. We are then reminded that Mr. Yeltsin is our best bet in Russia, and that withdrawal of the aid only would comfort his—and therefore our—enemies. ("His success is vital to the security of the West" claims the *New York Times*, July 5, 1993.) Accordingly, Mr. Yeltsin gets a second chance and further chances if need be. Until the day we emerge from Mr. Yeltsin's spell, placing conditions on Russian aid is just so much spin to fool the folks back home who foot the bill.

The futility of imposing conditionality on someone a good many Westerners—including the U.S. president and his close advisor Strobe Talbert—believe to be "vital to the security of the West" is exemplified in a *New York Times* editorial: "[A]fter victory in the April referendum, President Boris Yeltsin gained a measure of control. His Government has begun to cut back spending by raising energy prices and reducing subsidies to state-owned enterprises. And the central bank has raised interest rates and pledged to pull back on explosive increases in the money supply.

"These policies aren't yet tough enough—which is why the I.M.F. had previously refused to release aid. *But Mr. Yeltsin complained that without aid to ease the pain, he couldn't overcome opposition to tighter fiscal and monetary policies.* The United States agreed, urging the monetary fund to provide aid on the basis of the steps Mr. Yeltsin has already taken and those his Government has pledged for the future. Last week, the I.M.F. signed on."[19]

The IMF sign-on, or cave-in, should come as no surprise. And future sign-ons and cave-ins by an institution that preaches conditionality but too often practices capitulation when it comes to Boris Yeltsin no doubt are in store. "The Great Game," writes Steven Erlanger in the *New York Times*, "was what Kipling called the long struggle between the Russian and British empires over Central Asia. The great game these days is the struggle of the Russian Government to get loans out of the International Monetary Fund to bail out its budget. The pattern, as Western economists and diplomats have come to understand, is for the Russians to make plausible promises of fiscal and monetary discipline while citing the crucial importance of the success of Moscow's economic transformation to the well-being and peace of the world."[20]

Interestingly enough, the IMF has dropped all pretense that the purpose of its loans to Russia is other than to subsidize and prolong the political career of Boris Yeltsin. In a revealing admission to the *New York Times* about its 10.2 billion dollar loan to Russia just months before the June 1996 presidential elections in Russia, the head of the IMF, Michel Camdessus, argued "[The 10.2 billion dollar loan to Russia] can be seen and will be seen by many as betting on Yeltsin or a waste of money. But nothing more important could be done today for the prosperity of the entire world. So we must do it."[21]

"Although the monetary fund is not supposed to take sides in elections," write the two *New York Times* reporters who interviewed Camdessus, "the extraordinary deal—the second-largest loan in the fund's history—was driven by the West's desire to impede the comeback of the Communist Party in Russia. The United States and Germany urged that the loan be approved, but Mr. Camdessus had cleared the way by rewriting fund rules in 1994 to ease credit to Russia, and Mr. Camdessus went on Russian television to announce the largesse that Mr. Yeltsin's economic reforms had won."[22]

How can aid advocates seriously maintain that conditionality-guaranteed Western aid to Russia will be used for productive purposes when it has become apparent to all that the West believes it needs Boris Yeltsin at least as much as Yeltsin needs the West?

Even in circumstances where conditionality can be enforced, however, there is no reason to believe that the IMF will insist on the correct conditions. In an article entitled, "Mexicans Beware! What IMF Austerity Did for Venezuelans," economist Alejandro J. Sucre claims that "the economic consequences of [conditionality imposed by the IMF on Venezuela] could not have been more catastrophic. The per capita gross domestic product fell almost 8 percent from 1989 to 1993; the inflation index rose almost 10-fold; the outstanding foreign debt increased by $5 billion (mainly with the IMF and the World Bank); and the banking crisis that burst out in 1994 erased 10 percent of the GNP and $6 billion of the country's international reserves." [Alejandro J. Sucre, "Mexicans Beware! What IMF Austerity Did for Venezuelans."[23]

In return for loans to soften Venezuela's then-balance-of-payments crisis, the following conditions were imposed by the IMF under the guise of promoting a market economy: "a 168 percent devaluation of the bolivar as a result of the unqualified lifting of exchange controls; introduction of new taxes, including a 10 percent value added tax, a new assets tax, and a 3 percent surcharge on top of new inflation-adjusted taxes on the sale of certain assets (capital gains); raising the price of gasoline and other oil derivatives by as much as 110 percent; raising the public service rates of state-owned enterprises by an immediate 65 percent, with monthly incremental increases of 5 percent; raising of interest rates—real rates often shot above 40 percent; the reduction of tariffs on finished products; initiation of an unspecified privatization program and the 'restructuring' of some state-owned companies; and a rise in the minimum wage of 30 percent in bolivar terms."[24]

While each individual condition can be described as either good (tariff removal, exchange control removal), bad (raising the minimum wage) or horrendous (increasing taxes), their net effect resulted in substantial income transfer from the private sector of the economy to government. Writes Sucre: "The letter of intent that the Venezuelan government signed with the IMF—as well as its subsequent amendments—boiled down to a massive transfer of resources from the private sector to the pockets of the wasteful government. The government, at the IMF's behest, attempted to balance its accounts on the backs of the people—through devaluations, increased taxes and increased interest rates. All the focus was put on the fiscal demands of the state, but little or no attention was given to increasing the productive capacity of the nation. On the contrary, that capacity was diminished by the increasing scarcity of credit, reduced purchasing and saving capacity due to devaluations, and the increased costs of production due to rising taxes and government service charges. "[25]

The Venezuelan case illustrates the essential argument against foreign aid—that aid builds up the resources and influence of government even in circumstances when it is alleged to be necessary to promote a market economy.

In conclusion, there can be little doubt that the decade of the 90s has not been a good decade for foreign aid advocates. When Peter Bauer, Milton Friedman and myself wrote our separate attacks on foreign aid, we were called extremists. Yesterday's extremism, however, has become today's conventional wisdom. "The 1990s have proven a grim time for foreign aid as we know it—the grants and loans that are the traditional form of international development assistance," writes Howard W. French in the *New York Times*. "Everywhere these days, it seems, support for such aid is dwindling, and once-generous donors are focusing their energies inward. It hasn't been helpful, of course, that three decades of foreign development assistance in the third world has failed to lift the poorest of the poor in Africa and Asia much beyond where they have always been." (Howard W. French, "Donors of Foreign Aid Have Second Thoughts.")[26]

"[Many of the world's leading aid agencies] are beginning to suggest something that once was heard only from outright enemies of foreign aid: that big cash outlays to central governments may only pave the way to corruption. . . . In a research paper published last fall, Peter Boone, a professor at the London School of Economics, concluded that development assistance had fattened political elites and spawned a thriving global community of non-governmental organizations, but had done little to improve living standards in poor countries."[27]

It is now apparent that corruption could have been thwarted, hundreds of millions of foreign aid dollars saved, and most important, policies that have a higher probability of helping the poor nations than foreign aid effectuated, had the advice of the so-called "outright enemies of foreign aid" been heeded instead of ignored.

Economic Sanctions: The Opposite Side of the Coin

Foreign aid and economic sanctions are opposite sides of the same coin. Both seek to influence the behavior of foreign governments and, sometimes, their longevity as well. Economic aid are the carrots, and economic sanctions the sticks, of interventionist policy.

In theory, economic sanctions, actually imposed to change the behavior of a targeted country, cannot work. The target, after all, has a choice—either to capitulate before the sanctions are imposed and avoid their costs, or endure the sanctions. If the target perceives the costs of capitulation to be greater than the costs of the sanctions, the sanctions are imposed but will not work. On the other hand, if the sanctions' costs are perceived to be greater than the costs of capitulation, the target capitulates and the sanctions are not imposed. Two conclusions emerge from this analysis. The first is that sanctions, actually imposed, will not work unless, of course, the target misperceives costs and benefits. The second is that the *threat* of sanctions, if it is credible, may be useful in certain circumstances to change behavior.

The history of sanctions imposition confirms this theory. "Sanctions seldom change the policies of large, powerful countries, no matter how brilliantly implemented," writes trade expert Gary Hufbauer. "Midsized countries can also thwart sanctions, when local dictators are able to quell dissent with a powerful military and divert pain to citizens with no influence. . . . Even a small country can escape the punitive effects of sanctions if they are not enforced."[28]

Hufbauer cites three examples of sanctions that failed to change the policies of a powerful country. "U.S. sanctions did not influence Soviet policy in Afghanistan or Poland. Nor did the Soviet Union fare any better in changing Chinese ways by cutting off credits and technical assistance to China in the 1960s. U.S. sanctions against China following the Tiananmen Square massacre were similarly ineffective."[29]

Iraq is an example of a midsized country that has thwarted the effect of sanctions by diverting pain to citizens with no influence and by a leaky border with Jordan. Despite continuing U.N. sanctions, Saddam Hussein has outlasted his two chief tormenters during the Gulf War—George Bush and Margaret Thatcher.

Haiti is an example of a small country whose military government was able to escape the effects of sanctions that could not be enforced. "In Haiti, sanctions have been undermined by the porousness of the border with the Dominican Republic, whose president, Joaquin Balaguer, has long stated that he cannot control smuggling from his country. Even as new, more stringent measures took effect last week, ships loaded with embargoed fuel lined up in the Haitian port of Jacmel, having made the short trip from the Dominican Republic. And, of course, smuggling in the interior across the border, will be very hard to stop."[30]

The inability of sanctions to achieve desired results have been quantified by Hufbauer, Elliott and Schott.[31] Their conclusion:

"Sanctions failed to contribute to U.S. foreign policy objectives in 38 of 46 episodes between 1973 and 1990." These results contrast sharply to those of an earlier period—from the end of the Second World War to the early 1970s—when economic sanctions contributed to the achievement of U.S. foreign policy goals in eighteen of the thirty-five cases studied. The reason for the difference according to Hufbauer is declining U.S. economic leverage.

"By the 1970s, U.S. economic leverage was waning," writes Hufbauer. "Europe and Japan had recovered from the devastation of World War II and many developing countries were rapidly industrializing. With the global economy becoming increasingly open, there were more suppliers of goods, technology and finance, and many alternative markets. Countries targeted by American sanctions had choices—and they used them."[32]

Could there be a more convincing demonstration of declining U.S. economic leverage than President Clinton's failed attempt to wring human-rights concessions from the Chinese in return for extension by the U.S. of most favored nation (MFN) trading status? Throughout the MFN negotiations, Clinton acted as if he had the ace in the hole. But when push came to shove, it was the U.S. president who blinked, not the Chinese. In May 1996, the American president offered China unconditional MFN treatment even though China's human-rights record had not improved one iota.

Indeed, the fact that China is an authoritarian society that puts strict limits on dissent is a second reason U.S. threats of trade sanctions against China lack credibility. In a trade war, there are losers on both sides. If Chinese losers complain too vociferously, they will be silenced. American losers, on the other hand, can—and will—use the political process to press their case.

And a strong case it will be. A trade war with China—whether over human rights or Chinese pirating of U.S. hi-tech goods such as video and computer software—would be negative to U.S. interests from several points of view. First, trade sanctions cause an inefficient allocation of U.S. resources by restricting consumption and increasing inefficient domestic production of the sanctioned goods.

Second, we want to encourage free trade and other liberal economic policies in China. Trade sanctions encourage protectionism.

Third, we want to encourage pro-Western attitudes amongst Chinese leaders. Trade sanctions would reinforce existing Chinese paranoia about Western intentions.

Fourth, we want the United States to be seen as a reliable economic partner. Trade sanctions would demonstrate U.S. petulance and unreliability.

Finally, coming on the heals of the U.S. trade dispute with Japan, trade sanctions against China would encourage the view gaining force in Asia that the United States is a bully nation bent, in particular, on keeping Asian nations down. This could hurt us deeply in the entire region.

Declining fear of U.S. military might is yet another reason U.S. economic sanctions are not working. When the Dominicans openly defied the U.S. embargo on Haiti, for example, they demonstrated a lack of fear of U.S. military retaliation. Why should they be afraid? The reason President Clinton imposed the economic sanctions on Haiti in the first place was because he didn't want to use military force there. The same thing happened in Yugoslavia. There is an international trade embargo against the Serb economy, but it too has had little effect. Why? Because those who defy the embargo understand it exists only because the Western powers are unwilling to use force in the area.

The United States may have the strongest military machine in the world. But its reluctance to use force has meant that substitute measures, like economic sanctions—which often require some modicum of fear for their effective implementation—cannot work.

Indeed, not only do economic sanctions not work, but they actually can—and often do—enrich the very target they are designed to weaken. The purpose of U.S. sanctions against Haiti, for example, was to depose the military government there. But they had an opposite effect—they enriched the military dictators at the expense of ordinary Haitian citizens. A simple economics lesson explains how this happened.

When the United States embargoed fuel into Haiti, its price inside Haiti dramatically rose by comparison with its world price. As a result, monopoly profits could be made by buying fuel at the world price and selling it at the Haitian price. Those allowed to make this profitable trade were friends of the military dictators whom, one may presume, paid handsomely for the privilege.

"In what is widely considered one of the most flagrant examples [of war profiteering]," writes the *New York Times* correspondent in Haiti, "the Mevs family has reportedly been building a huge oil depot here to help the army defy the embargo. 'Right in the middle of the embargo, you have a guy who is described by the Americans as a friend getting a contract like this' said one Haitian businessman. 'The joke is that these people are being allowed to profit grotesquely from the sanctions.'"[33] Those who "suffer grotesquely," on the other hand, are ordinary Haitians whose living standard declines because of the high price and limited availability of fuel.

A similar story has played out in Serbia. Roger Thurow of the *Wall Street Journal* filed the following report on June 7, 1994 from Belgrade.

> The Serbs, it would seem, have pulled off the economic miracle of the ages.
>
> Inflation, which at the beginning of the year was doubling every several hours, is now next to nothing. The dinar, as worthless as old gum wrappers a few months ago, is now pegged by the government to equal the German mark. And stores, once barren, now offer a dazzling array of imports, from Pampers to Air Jordans. All this in a country supposedly ravaged by three years of war in neighboring Croatia and Bosnia-Herzegovina and an international trade embargo.
>
> "How do we do it?" asks the Yugoslav central bank director, Dragoslav Avramovic. "It's 90% luck, 10% wits."
>
> And a whole lot of help from an international criminal underworld.
>
> Although the government has restrained spending and stopped round-the-clock printing of money, its newfound fiscal discipline is being propped up by a veritable army of pickpockets, drug dealers, smugglers, extortionists and gangsters at work throughout Europe. In essence, the gangs generate the cash and commodities needed to keep this Serb-dominated country and its war effort in Bosnia afloat.
>
> The thievery and scams provide a constant flow of foreign currency into the country that is vital to the government's effort to support the dinar. And the smuggling of everything from oil and weapons to cigarettes and pork chops has relieved the government of having to finance sanctions-busting imports, an activity that originally helped push inflation to dizzying heights.
>
> All of this has, up to now, blunted the sting of United Nations sanctions and created an illusion of plenty in an otherwise impoverished land, allowing President Slobodan Milosevic to stave off social unrest and remain all-powerful despite deafening international condemnation.
>
> *Government ministers indignantly reject the suspicions of Western police and diplomats that the government is in cahoots with the criminals, who the ministers say are controlled by paramilitary leaders or mobsters.* Mirko Marjanovic, the new prime minister, says he is a crusader against what he calls "war profiteers." Yet as he speaks, he proudly offers a visitor smuggled Kent cigarettes and his secretary pours a glass of scotch. "Twelve-year-old Chivas Regal," Mr. Marjanovic says. "You can buy it here in the stores."[34]

Despite their record of punishing the poor and failing to topple dictators in such diverse countries as Haiti, Cuba, Iraq, Vietnam,

North Korea, and Iran, economic sanctions remain the weapon of choice for interventionists who want to do something against their favorite villains abroad, but prefer not to use military force.[35] Their rallying cry has become: "economic sanctions worked in South Africa, didn't they?"—to which the correct answer is, no they did not. True, economic sanctions were imposed against South Africa and, true, the hateful regime of apartheid did fall. But if ever there was a case where correlation did not prove cause and effect, South Africa was that case.

Just as with other countries, economic sanctions against South Africa punished South Africa's poor more than its elites. Why such redistribution would pressure the elites to abandon apartheid—a policy they supposedly supported—is something of a mystery. After all, economic sanctions—and severe ones at that—did not cause Castro to give up communism, Saddam Hussein to give up Baathist totalitarianism, and Slobodan Milosevic to give up ethnic cleansing. One must ask oneself why economic sanctions would work in one case and no other.

Indeed, rather than hasten apartheid's demise, it is likely that economic sanctions actually retarded it. There's one school of thought that South Africa's elite already had become disenchanted with apartheid by the time the sanctions were imposed in 1986 and were angling for a negotiated settlement. But South Africa's political leaders—particularly the truculent P. W. Botha—did not want to be seen to be acting from weakness. Former U.S. Ambassador to South Africa Herman Nickel writes: "With United States encouragement, Justice Minister Kobie Coetsee sought permission from P. W. Botha in 1985 to accept Nelson Mandela's offer to start talking. If anything, these talks were dealt a setback by the 1986 sanctions vote, since P. W. Botha never wanted to be seen to act from weakness and reverted to his repressive, counterrevolutionary mode."[36]

"Anthony Lewis [who argues that sanctions hastened apartheid's fall] notes . . . the important part Sir Robin Renwick played in encouraging President F. W. de Klerk to release Nelson Mandela and facilitating negotiations," continues Nickel. "But Mr. Lewis misses the salient point behind Sir Robin's extraordinary effectiveness. He would never have been able to play this role had he not represented a government that steadfastly resisted sanctions. This is what allowed the British to retain the access and influence in Pretoria that United States diplomacy effectively lost the moment Congress overrode Ronald Reagan's sanctions veto in October 1986."

P. W. Botha's own words support Nickel's interpretation. Following President Reagan's imposition of sanctions, Botha wrote in the *Washington Post*: "Whatever the intention, the effect is punitive. It is a negative step. Cooperation should not be based on coercion. Such actions diminish the ability of the United States to influence events in southern Africa."[37]

What accounts, then, for the successful negotiated dismantling of apartheid in South Africa? According to Ambassador Nickel, "two unpredictable events dramatically accelerated the timetable for South Africa's negotiated revolution. The first was that in 1989 P. W. Botha suffered a stroke, giving an increasingly restive National Party the chance to rid itself of his oppressive yoke, and to install F. W. de Klerk in his place.

"The second was the Soviet empire's sudden implosion. This allowed Mr. de Klerk to remove the National Party's bogyman of the 'total onslaught' as an obstacle to legalizing and negotiating with the A.N.C. and its formal ally, the South African Communist Party. Mercifully, it discredited the A.N.C.'s socialist role model."[38]

In conclusion, economic sanctions have become a serious source of loss for the United States. The benefits have been minimal in terms of achieving U.S. foreign-policy objectives, while their economic costs for the U.S. have been substantial. When the U.S. boycotts Cuba, for example, U.S. consumers lose because they can't import Cuban goods (such as genuine Havana cigars), and U.S. exporters lose because they can't sell their wares to Cuban consumers. U.S. investors also lose because they are prevented from investing in Cuba.

Sanctions also can threaten trade relations with allies who do not go along with U.S. sanctions. The U.S. knows, for example, that one reason its sanctions against Fidel Castro have not worked is because our allies, including our NAFTA partners, trade with and invest in Cuba. Bill Clinton has tried to persuade our trading partners to cut their trade links with Cuba, but they refuse. They have their own foreign policies to pursue, they argue, and these do not include boycotting Cuba.

In July 1996, President Clinton (who, after all, championed the formation of NAFTA) publicly threatened Mexico and Canada: either stop doing business with Cuba, or the U.S. will impose economic sanctions against *you*. Writes the *New York Times*: "Last week President Clinton said he would allow the most sweeping provision of the Helms-Bentin bill—which penalizes foreign businesses that invest in property that the Castro government confiscated from current American citizens—to take effect. But he delayed enforcement for six months."[39]

Many observers believe Bill Clinton's threats against our trading partners were empty ones—made only to win the votes of Cubans in Florida. Now that he is reelected, the economic sanctions against our NAFTA partners are highly unlikely. Still, Canada and Mexico are deeply—and quite justifiably—offended by Clinton's attacks on their national sovereignty. NAFTA, after all, is only a free-trade agreement. In no way does it imply that Canada and Mexico adopt U.S. foreign policies. The bottom line: if Bill Clinton's purpose is to destroy the basic fabric of NAFTA, there are few better ways of doing this than threatening Canada and Mexico with economic sanctions if they fail to support U.S. foreign-policy initiatives.

6

The Consensus of Expert Opinion

It is hard to overestimate the damage socialist fallacies have done to the poor nations of the world. Import substitution and big government tax and spending policies have proved ruinous to these countries—yet these were the very policies the "experts" promised the poor would lead them out of their poverty. "The LDCs are caught in the vicious circle of poverty," wrote the young Walter Heller in 1964. "To break out of this circle, apart from foreign aid, calls for vigorous taxation and government development programs; on this point expert opinion is nearing a consensus."[1]

Indeed it was. And Western universities—particularly the prestigious ones—played a major role in formulating and disseminating the "consensus of expert opinion." When Heller at Minnesota, John Kenneth Galbraith and Richard Musgrave at Harvard, Nicholas Kaldor at Cambridge University in England, and Gunnar Myrdal, wherever the peripetic social philosopher happened to be, revealed to their students that big government was the savior, the gullible, innocent, and naive—many from the less-developed world—hurried to join the church. "The nineteenth-century sequence will probably not be repeated," wrote Norman S. Buchanan. "The state rather than the drive of private enterprise in pursuit of profits will determine the major features of industrial development in the [now] low income areas. Domestic savings and investment, labor training and mobility, imports and exports, foreign borrowing and home finance will be guided by the visible hand of the state in the quest for higher incomes through industrialization. "[2]

Gunnar Myrdal couldn't agree more with Professor Buchanan's predictions. In 1954 he wrote, "All special advisers to underdeveloped countries who have taken the time and trouble to acquaint themselves with the problems, no matter who they are—teams of experts from the International Bank or other international agencies, including the Colombo Plan; officials of the American Point Four Program; private foundations and consultant firms; independent social scientists; journalists or visiting politicians—all recommend central planning as a first condition for progress. Implicitly they all assume a different approach to the social and economic problems of the underdeveloped countries today than that which historically was applied in the advanced countries. *They all assume a very much greater role for the state.* "[3]

Indeed they did—and my how times have changed. Today, slightly more than forty years after Myrdal published these words, the pendulum has swung a full 180 degrees in the opposite direction. Virtually all scholars and statesmen support a smaller role for the state in the development process than forty years ago. And the reason has less to do with ideology than economic performance. "Development has worked above all in east Asia," writes Martin Wolf in the *Financial Times*, "[and] these countries have best conformed to the 'Washington consensus' of fiscal conservatism, outward-orientation and reliance on market forces. "[4]

Cart-Before-the-Horse Economics

A prime tenet of the "consensus of expert opinion" in the 1950s, '60s, and '70s is that so-called "social overhead capital," or infrastructure, must lead the development process. According to Richard and Peggy Musgrave: "Particularly in the early stages of development, public sector investment is of critical importance since, in the form of so-called infrastructure (power, communications, port facilities, roads, etc.), it sets the framework for subsequent manufacturing investment whether public or private. Furthermore, capital formation includes investment in human resources in the form of education and training as well as in physical assets. Indeed, where human productivity is adversely affected by malnutrition and disease, increased food consumption and the provision of sanitation and health facilities take on the aspect of investment in human capital. "[5]

The central role assigned to "social overhead capital" or infrastructure in the development process by the "consensus of expert opinion" represented the victory of social-democratic ideology—in particular, the desire to provide an excuse for big government in the poorer countries—over sound economic analysis. Heller lets the cat out of the bag when he writes: "Perhaps the most striking feature of the capital formation process in the underdeveloped economy is the large and inescapable role that government must play in providing 'social overhead capital' both as a direct instrument of economic development and as a prerequisite to increased participation of private capital in the development process. A brief consideration of the relationship of these types of investment to the development process will make clear why governments of underdeveloped countries have to play such a central role in the capital formation process and why, in turn, the strengthening of the tax system to yield adequate revenues is of such primary concern."[6]

But doesn't Heller understand that the high taxes needed to finance the social-overhead capital, by restricting private economic activity, obviates the need for the very infrastructure the taxes finance? One wonders: What good are roads if the taxes needed to finance them restricts business and with it the demand for transportation facilities? What good are modern port facilities if the demand for their services is curtailed by bad business brought about by high taxes? Indeed, what good is any form of costly infrastructure if there is scant demand for its services?

Putting the cart before the horse—by raising taxes to finance the infrastructures of stagnant economies—only guarantees there will be empty roads and underused port facilities in societies that can ill afford the waste.

This is essentially the conclusion reached by Albert O. Hirschman in *The Strategy of Economic Development*.[7] Hirschman distinguishes between "development via shortage of social overhead capital" and "development via excess capacity of social overhead capital." If we endow an underdeveloped country with a first-class highway network, with extensive hydro electric and perhaps irrigation facilities," he writes, "can we be certain that industrial and agricultural activity will expand in the wake of these improvements? Would it not be less risky and more economical first to make sure of such activity . . . and then let the ensuing pressures determine the appropriate outlays for social overhead capital and its location? . . . To place one's faith in purely permissive sequences and to rely on the ability of infrastructure facilities to call forth other economic activities can . . . be just as irrational as the so-called 'Cargo Cult' that had been engaged in by some of the New Guinea tribes after the lamented departure of the Allied expeditionary force at the end of World War II: 'Those in the coastal villages have built wharves out into the sea, ready for the ships to tie up, and those in land villages have constructed airstrips out of the jungle for the planes to land. And they waited in expectancy for the Second Coming of the Cargoes!' Touching as it is, such a belief in the propitiatory powers of social overhead capital should not be the basis of development policy."[8]

Hirschman's argument, to be sure, is not that social-overhead capital has no role to play in the development process—only that infrastructure should follow rather than lead private economic growth. "Rapidly growing centers will usually suffer shortages," writes Hirschman, "sometimes because of lack of proper planning, but often also because it would be illegitimate and wasteful to expand infrastructure facilities in anticipation of the kind of extremely rapid economic progress that does hit a city or area sometimes, but whose occurrence or continuation can never be predicted with confidence. When these shortages do occur, they do not seem to affect the growth perceptibly, but rather are taken as an additional proof that dynamic development is indeed under way. In an underdeveloped country it is often the city with the worst water, power, and housing shortages that is most favored by private investors."[9]

"Infrastructure first," then, not only is bad economics, but, from a historical point of view, it is not the way development actually proceeded in the real world. "It is not true," writes Peter Bauer, "that a substantial infrastructure is a precondition for development. The suggestion that a ready-made infrastructure is necessary for development ignores the fact that the infrastructure develops in the course of economic progress, not ahead of it. The suggestion is yet another example of an unhistorical and unrealistic attitude to the process of development. Much of the literature suggests that the world was somehow created in two parts: one part with a ready-made infrastructure of railways, roads, ports, pipelines and public utilities, which has therefore been able to develop, and the other which the creator unfortunately forgot to endow with social overhead capital. This is not the way things happened."[10]

The Egalitarian Lie

It is bad enough when economists give bad advice because the theories upon which the advice is based turn out to be faulty. It is far worse when the economists' bad advice results from the misuse of scientific authority to impose their own moral values on others.

For example, Walter Heller's extreme statement in 1964 that "many LDCs [less developed contries] are characterized by extremes of wealth and poverty which, in terms of the egalitarian ethic as accepted throughout the free world, constitute a compelling case for redistributive government finance," would be dismissed as pure bunk if the man was not wrapped in scientific robes. In 1964, there was no such egalitarian ethic accepted throughout the free world. Yet many naive persons accepted Heller's dictum as scientific truth simply because Heller had a considerable scientific reputation.

So strong was its attachment to egalitarian values, that the expert consensus made redistribution of income and wealth a precondition for economic progress in the poorer countries even though the experts really knew better. For example, Myrdal, the egalitarian ideologue, claims that "no national integration and no economic progress is possible without vast redistributional reforms." Yet, Myrdal, the economist, betrays his egalitarian ideological biases when, on the very same page, he admits "in these [poor] countries where capital formation is so necessary and has such severe limitations because of the great poverty, an unequal distribution could be defended with more justification than in our rich and industrially advanced countries as having the social functions of creating savings."[11]

Myrdal, the egalitarian ideologue, favors progressive taxation in the poor countries because "their tax systems are regularly regressive and, in particular, spare the rich from any considerable burden." Yet the economist in him warns tax collectors "to tread this road with utmost care in order not to destroy the forces for economic development."

Make no mistake about it. As economists *qua* economists, the consensus of expert opinion was not incompetent—that's what gave credibility to their policy advice. Myrdal understood the negative incentive effects of progressive taxation—and he knew that high-income individuals accounted for the majority of the poor country's savings. But by letting their egalitarian, big-government ideology run roughshod over their economics, the consensus betrayed both their metier and the poor people whose interests they claimed to have in mind.

On this latter point, Peter Bauer deserves special praise for calling Myrdal on the carpet: "Although [Myrdal's] books abound in sympathetic references to the plight of the underdeveloped countries, there is nevertheless a distinct ambiguity towards the beneficiaries of Professor Myrdal's proposals. He [Myrdal] writes: 'Not merely to save the world, but primarily to save our own souls, there should again be dreamers, planners, and fighters, in the midst of our nations, who would take upon themselves the important social function in democracy of raising our sights—so far ahead that their proponents again form a definite minority in their nations and avoid the unbearable discomfort for reformers of a climate of substantial agreement.' But the price to be paid by others may be too high for the salvation of even the most ardent souls, if interpersonal comparisons of utility and cost may be permitted on this occasion."[12]

It is, of course, a bold and dangerous lie to claim—as Myrdal does—that no economic progress is possible without vast redistributional reforms. If anything, the history of the development process indicates the opposite. There is, of course, Nobel Prize winner Simon Kuznets's empirical observation that income and wealth inequality is associated with dramatic economic progress in the early stages of the development process, with income becoming more equalized as development proceeds (the so-called "U-curve"). Moreover, there is evidence that vast redistributional reforms, when they are imposed, serve to retard rather than accelerate economic growth.

"Inequality of wealth," writes Peter Bauer, "is not an obstacle to economic advance. For example, the wealth of the Chinese immigrants of south-east Asia, to take just one obvious example already instanced in this volume, which implies a high degree of economic inequality conventionally measured, has obviously not retarded economic advance. It reflects largely the result of the performance of economic services and the fruits of saving and of reinvestment of profits. The prospects of higher incomes and of the possibility of accumulating wealth have attracted enterprising people of various races to south-east Asia and elicited a supply of productive effort, enterprise, saving and investment. Countless other examples can be listed, including the activities of Jews, Japanese, Greeks, Indians, Levantines and Europeans in many parts of the world."[13]

In a similar vein, my colleague at the Hoover Institution, Thomas Sowell, writes: "High productivity may contribute greatly to the material well-being, physical health, and cultural opportunities of a nation, and yet those responsible for that productivity may be resented, hated, and attacked both politically and physically. Down through the centuries and around the world, the bearers of the skills and disciplines that bring economic progress have been viewed as people whose prosperity has come at the expense of others. The repeated history of economic losses suffered by nations that expelled them has yet to teach a permanent lesson to the contrary.

"Those who have created economic enterprises are depicted politically as having 'taken over' or 'monopolized' economic activities that existed somehow. Their share in the additional output they created is depicted as a net loss to the economy, especially if any of it is spent in another country. Thus the Indians of East Africa have been said to have acquired a "stranglehold" on the commerce and industry of that region—as if that commerce and industry existed independently of the Indians and simply fell victim to their malign influence. Much the same vision has been applied to the work of the overseas Chinese, the Jews, the Armenians, and others. The economic benefits created have been taken for granted, while the special prosperity of particular classes, nations, or ethnic groups who have established the industry and commerce from which these economic benefits flow have come to be regarded as suspicious, or as demonstrably sinister."[14]

Sowell's point, of course, is that a good part of income inequality reflects inequality in economic productivity, so that the vast redistributional reforms desired by Myrdal and his egalitarian cohorts necessarily imply reduced economic growth—paid less, either the high-productivity groups produce less or escape to more hospitable climes. Needless to say, the egalitarian ideologues did not see it this way or, what may be closer to the truth, refused to allow themselves to see it this way. Instead, they argue redistribution increases economic productivity and growth if the higher taxes on the more productive are used to finance education and health services for the less productive. "To the extent that taxation finances the process of human capital formation at the expense of lavish consumption, speculation and foreign exchange hoarding rather than at the expense of productive private investment," writes Heller, "it increases productivity and accelerates development."[15]

Myrdal concurs with Heller: "A determined drive for educational reform on a broad front, stretching from a general literacy drive to the widening and modernization of training centers on the university level, will not be inexpensive. As has often been observed, this type of consumption is productive; it is really capital formation, though invested in people and not in the material tools for production. . . . The same is true in regard to health. Productivity is kept down by preventable illness. But again, the question of the most remunerative direction of efforts is a crucial one in the underdeveloped countries whose only chance of economic development depends upon the most careful husbandry of scarce resources. And again, it is a question of overcoming vested interests, rooted in the great economic inequalities in these countries and in the class structure."[16]

Note should be taken that the "human capital" argument for high taxes on economically productive citizens advanced by Myrdal, Heller, and other social democrats suffers from a similar deficiency as the "infrastructure first" argument for high taxes discussed above. Because imposing high taxes on the economically productive chokes off private business activity that provides jobs for workers, the so-called investment in human capital does not turn out to be investment at all. True, the masses can be expected to be healthier because of better nutrition and sanitation. And they also may acquire new skills in schools. This is all to the good.

But if there are no jobs because redistributive finance has chased domestic savings out of the poor country and frightened off foreign investment, the masses may not be able to cash in on their improved health and skills. What is billed as investment in human capital in these circumstances will be nothing more than standard-style, welfare-state social spending of the type that Myrdal himself decries as inappropriate to the limited circumstance of the poorer countries. "The advanced countries had very little of redistributional social security systems until they had reached a much higher level of productivity," warns Myrdal the economist.[17]

The argument that high taxes to finance education and health can backfire does not mean, of course, that poor countries should ignore education and health. On the contrary. Empirical studies show growth rates tend to be higher when there is investment in human capital and lower when there is unproductive government spending. For example, Singapore, Hong Kong, Taiwan, South Korea, ... , etc. all have put considerable resources into education—particularly primary and secondary education—and all have excellent records of economic performance, practicing what might be called "preventive" as opposed to "remedial" income redistribution.

The point, however, is that the East Asian economies do not finance their human capital with high taxes; they finance all their capital formation—human as well as physical—with economic growth. Low taxes spur high growth—high growth, in turn, generates substantial tax *revenues* from modest tax *rates*. The benefits of this East Asian approach, by comparison with egalitarianism, is obvious. Spending on education and health in East Asia truly is *investment* in human capital. Spending on education and health, financed by high tax rates, often turns out to be public *consumption*.

Another example where "preventive" income redistribution financed primary and secondary education is Indonesia. When oil prices soared in the late seventies, oil exporters found themselves flushed with surplus funds. Some like Nigeria squandered the oil windfall by building a new capital city; others like Saudi Arabia built lavish monuments, purchased weapons, practiced conspicuous consumption and so on. But Indonesia had the good sense to spend the money wisely—on primary and secondary education. Little wonder then that Indonesia has averaged 6 percent annual economic growth for the last quarter of a century.

An aside: social democrats like Heller, Musgrave, and Myrdal often use code words like "lavish consumption," "speculation," and "foreign exchange hoarding" to justify the taxation of high-income and high-net-worth individuals in the less-developed countries. All three practices, however, have a common root—lack of faith in the local currency because of the monetary and fiscal impropriety of the public authorities. Expected explosions of the money supply due to deficit financing, for example, lead people who have the ability to save actually to save less, and consume more, to escape the expected erosion in the real value of savings. It also leads to foreign-exchange accumulation and hoarding by locals to escape the expected depreciation of the local currency. Clearly, it is as wrong to penalize the intended victims of inflation for trying to protect themselves from public irresponsibility as it would be to penalize the intended victim of a mugging for trying to escape its undesirable consequences. If the egalitarian economists really were serious about curbing excessive consumption and foreign-exchange hoarding, they would have advised the public authorities in the poorer countries to cut back on their inflationary-financed government spending, not increase it.

Because the egalitarian economists tailored their economics to their ideological beliefs, there are important missing pieces in their analysis of the development process. Myrdal, for instance, stressed the importance to development of generating increasing amounts of domestic savings, but appeared oblivious to the obvious likelihood that income and wealth redistribution would drive the savings—and savers—to more hospitable climes. Even more important would be the impediment egalitarian measures impose on incoming foreign investment. One of the most important reasons East Asian economic development has gone so well has been the ability of the Asian economies to attract foreign investment. Fiscal conservatism, outward-oriented trade policies, and a general reliance on market forces have been the attractions. But would foreign capital have been as willing to locate in these countries if they had engaged in vigorous egalitarian finance? Of course not!

By stressing egalitarianism and downplaying incentives, the consensus of expert opinion effectively undermined the hopes of the poorer countries for rapid and sustained economic development.

Perhaps the most grievous omission from the consensus analysis of the development process was that of property rights. It is not surprising egalitarians and anti-capitalists would overlook property rights as an important determinant of economic growth—their ideology could not have it otherwise. But the victory for ideology proved a crushing defeat for science—at least the science of the expert consensus. "Statistical analysis of data from about 100 countries from 1960 to 1990 reveals a number of variables that influence the growth rate of real GDP per head," writes economist Robert Barro. "The growth rate tends to be higher if the government protects property rights, maintains free markets and spends little on non-productive consumption. Also helpful are high levels of human capital in the forms of education and health, and low fertility rates.

"If two countries pursue similar policies, the country that starts with a lower level of real GDP per head is likely to grow faster. In other words, if a poor country can maintain good policies and accumulate a reasonable level of human capital, then it tends to catch up with the richer countries (as has happened with east Asian tigers such as South Korea and Taiwan). However, countries are likely to remain poor if their governments distort markets and fail to maintain property rights."[18]

Agricultural reform in China is a specific and powerful example of the critical role property rights play in economic development process. The decollectivization of agriculture in China happened more or less spontaneously, beginning in 1978 with experiments in the poorest areas of some provinces, and lasting until 1983 when the last agricultural communes disappeared. Household agriculture replaced the commune system as land was leased to peasants by government for a maximum of fifteen years.

The result of decollectivization was a dramatic and largely one-shot increase in agricultural productivity. From 1978 to 1984, agricultural output grew at five times the rate of the preceding twenty years, while farm income and consumption grew even more rapidly. This can be called a "property rights" effect. When the peasants acquired the rights to the crops they grew, they grew more crops.

Property rights also explain why the dramatic increase in the rate of agricultural productivity could not be sustained after 1984.

Because the peasants did not acquire the land they farmed, they did not have the incentive to make the necessary investments and improvements. "The incomplete nature of property rights in rural China has had a negative impact on agriculture's performance," writes Dwight Perkins. "Because farmers weren't secure that they would keep their property, even over the 15-year lease, they were reluctant to invest in major capital improvements, particularly land improvements such as irrigation systems. ... The inability to sell land meant that farmers wishing to migrate to urban areas continued to hold onto their land, farming that land using their spare time or elderly relatives simply to maintain their rights."[19]

A Special Case?

As discussed in an earlier chapter, the early welfare states were free traders, at least as far as trade between the advanced industrial economies were concerned. But while they believed in open trade policies for their own countries, the consensus of expert opinion treated the poorer nations as a special case where the normal rules of proper conduct did not apply. "When economists, without explicitly accounting for it, treat the commercial policy problems of underdeveloped countries within the framework of general themes that are fitted to the conditions and interests of the advanced countries," writes Myrdal, "they are following a procedure which is intellectually false.[20]

This central idea of the consensus of expert opinion, that the poorer countries are in some fundamental sense different from the advanced industrial ones such that the fundamental laws of economics do not apply to them—or that the poorer countries, because of their particular situation, are excused from these laws—has led to major policy mistakes and economic damage to those least able to afford it. For just as the law of gravity applies to all individuals—tall and short, fat and thin—the law of comparative advantage applies to all countries—big or small, rich or poor. The fact that, from an institutional point of view, comparative advantage manifests itself differently in a poor Latin American country than a rich North American one is an irrelevancy that in no way negates the law's fundamental truth—that a global system of specialization and interdependence benefits poor and rich countries alike.

No country is exempt from the law of comparative advantage— and those that have tried to exempt themselves have paid dearly for their transgressions.

Notwithstanding this basic truth, the third tenet of the consensus of expert opinion was import protection. "In addition . . . to this immediate reason for applying import restrictions, in order to preserve the foreign exchange balance," writes Myrdal, "the underdeveloped countries have quite a number of other sound reasons, *based on their peculiar situation*, for using [import] restriction for protective purposes."[21] "The four special reasons for industrial protection in underdeveloped countries [are] the difficulties of finding demand to match new supply, the existence of surplus labor, the large rewards of industrial investments in creating external economies, and the lopsided internal price structure disfavoring industry."[22]

As subsequent research by many scholars, including Gottfried Haberler, Harry G. Johnson, and Jagdish Bhagwati, has shown, none of Myrdal's so-called "four special reasons" for protection stand up to rigorous analysis. Consider the argument that protection is needed to provide demand for new supply. Import restrictions raise the price of imported goods in the protecting country, causing a diversion of demand from low-cost foreign to high-cost local sources of supply. This does increase domestic output of import substitutes but at the expense of reduced output of other sectors as resources are reallocated from more efficient to less efficient uses. This involves waste and a reduced living standard for the country as a whole.

Wasting resources in countries that have precious few resources to begin with clearly is not in the best interests of poor countries. Indeed, the whole idea of artificially pumping up demand for "new supply" is wrongheaded. If local producers can make decent goods at decent prices, demand will take care of itself. If they can't, the local producers can be helped only at a substantial cost to the overall economy.

Myrdal's argument in favor of protection of local industries that yield external economics to other domestic industries also is mistaken. If there are indeed external economies attached to a local industry—and the likelihood of misrepresentation to obtain favorable treatment is great here—the proper method of exploiting them is to subsidize the production yielding the externalities, not impose an import restriction. The import restriction is equivalent to a tax on consumption combined with a subsidy to production. Since only the subsidy to production is needed to exploit the assumed externality, the tax on consumers constitutes an unnecessary cost.

The argument that protection is the best way to employ surplus labor in a poor country is even weaker than the external economy argument. "Probably the most famous paper in all of development economics," writes economist Paul Krugman, "is Arthur Lewis's 'Economic development with unlimited supplies of labor.' In retrospect, it is hard to see exactly why. One interpretation of Lewis's argument is that the shadow price of labor drawn from the agricultural sector in developing countries is zero or at least low, so that the social return to investment in industry exceeds its private return. It was pretty obvious even early on, however, that this was a fragile basis on which to justify protection and promotion of industry."[23]

The surplus labor problem may be peculiar to poorer countries but the rule for solving it—no subsidy without externality—is a general rule applicable to rich and poor alike.

Today there can be little doubt that the protectionist prescriptions of the expert consensus constituted malpractice of the highest order. It is admittedly difficult to obtain definitive answers to many economic questions but the one that seems most robust is the contribution international trade makes to economic growth. In an empirical study of 119 countries, Ross Levine and David Renelt make the following point: "A vast literature uses cross-country regressions to search for empirical linkages between long-run growth rates and a variety of economic policy, political, and institutional indicators. This paper examines whether the conclusions from existing studies are robust or fragile to small changes in the conditioning information set. We find that almost all results are fragile. We do, however, identify a positive, robust correlation between growth and the share of investment in GDP and between the investment share and the ratio of international trade to GDP."[24]

In other words, Levine and Renelt find that one of the few sure things one can say about growth is that, under a wide variety of circumstances, high growth rates and high ratios of trade to GDP are closely linked.

Is Democracy Good For Growth?

One way to interpret the social-welfare state is as a sort of luxury good. Rich countries consume more social-welfare type activities for their own intrinsic value even though they have an adverse effect on economic growth. Rich countries apparently feel they can afford the reduced rate of economic progress. Robert Barro, in an analysis of how political democracy affects economic growth, adopts a similar interpretation for political democracy.[25] "One way to view the findings," writes Barro, "is that political freedom emerges as a sort of luxury good. Rich places consume more democracy because this good is desirable for its own sake and even though the increased political freedom may have an adverse effect on growth."

"The data reveal a stronger linkage between economic development and the propensity to experience democracy. Non-democratic countries that have achieved high standards of living—measured by real per-capita GDP, life expectancy and schooling—tend to become more democratic over time. Examples include Chile, South Korea, Taiwan, Spain and Portugal. Conversely, democratic countries with low standards of living tend to lose political rights over time. Examples include most of the newly independent African states in the 1970s."[26]

Unlike social democracy, however—whose effect on economic growth is both unambiguous and negative—the effect of political democracy on growth is *a priori* indeterminate. "Theoretically, writes Barro, "the effect of more democracy on growth is ambiguous. The negative effects involve the tendency to enact rich-to-poor redistributions of income (including land reforms) under majority voting and the enhanced role of interest groups in systems with representative legislatures. On the other side, democratic institutions provide a check of governmental power and thereby limit the potential of public officials to amass personal wealth and to carry out unpopular (and perhaps unproductive) projects.

". . . The analysis has implications for the desirability of exporting democratic institutions from the advanced Western countries to developing nations. Democracy is not the key to economic growth, and political freedoms tend to erode over time if they are out of line with a country's standard of living. Specifically, the U.S. plan to establish democracy in Haiti is a counterproductive policy. It will not improve the standard of living—the main problem in a poor country—and the democracy will almost surely be temporary."

"More generally, the advanced Western countries would contribute more to the welfare of poor nations by exporting their economic systems, notable property rights and free markets, rather than their political systems, which typically developed after reasonable standards of living had been attained. If economic freedom were to be established in a poor country, then growth would be encouraged, and the country would tend eventually to become more democratic on its own. Thus, in the long run, the propagation of Western-style economic systems would also be the effective way to expand democracy in the world."[27]

The New Orthodoxy

The wrongheadedness and utter ineptitude of the policies recommended by the left-wing orthodoxy of the 1950s is recognized today even by those who feel the development-policy pendulum may be swinging too much in the opposite direction. Krugman writes, for example: "Another embarrassment for development has been the realization of the extent to which the rhetoric of development theory has been used to cover poorly conceived or even corrupt policies. . . . The calculation of effective rates of protection, whatever the method's flaws, revealed rates of protection that were often absurdly high, some cases of negative value-added at world prices, and highly variable rates of protection across industries that were hard to justify. Country studies of trade policy revealed a heavy preference for complex administrative regulations that were evidently more costly than tariffs, and failed to yield revenue. Studies of repressed financial systems showed similar irrationalities. And it became apparent that the incentives provided by administratively generated rents were becoming major objectives both of legal and illegal economic activity."[28]

Krugman then observes that a new orthodoxy has come to replace the old one. "These observations of bad policies based on old development economics provided a key argument in what amounted to the formation of a new orthodoxy," writes Krugman.". . . It is certainly true that in the 1950s market failures were seen as pervasive and the case for intervention was taken not to be not so much an empirical observation as an obviously true conclusion from obviously true theory. By around 1980 a belief in the efficacy of free trade and free markets for developing countries had similarly taken hold, its intellectual credibility underpinned by neoclassical general equilibrium theory's demonstration of market efficiency. This orthodoxy also in effect denies that there is anything special about the situation of less developed countries compared with those of richer nations. The poor are no different from you and me—they just make less money."[29]

Will this new orthodoxy, based on free trade and free markets, turn out as unsatisfactory as the old? Krugman preaches caution: "don't get caught up too much in the orthodoxy of the moment," he warns. "We should keep at least in the back of our minds the thought that it is not true that economic theory 'proves' that free markets are always best: there is an intellectually solid case for some government industry promotion, one which has often seemed empirically plausible to sophisticated observers."[30]

But what Krugman's warnings overlook is that the new orthodoxy is not based on economic theory. Rather it is based on the cold
facts of experience—on what actually happened in Hong Kong,
Singapore, South Korea, Taiwan, indeed all over East Asia. In these
societies, essential reliance on market forces, liberal trade and capital-
import policies, fiscal conservatism, macroeconomic stability, and
low taxes produced extraordinary economic progress. This is what
gives the new orthodoxy its strength and credibility—not theoretical
arguments, however elegant and cogent they may be.

Similarly, what did in the old orthodoxy was not neoclassical
general equilibrium theory, but the wretchedness of those economies
who were either unfortunate or unwise enough to put the old orthodoxy into practice. Nothing succeeds like success in this world and,
in the case of the old consensus of expert opinion, nothing failed like
failure. Today, the only controversy remaining over the proper role of
the state in the development process concerns industrial policy. To
be sure, none of East Asia's success stories followed the Hong Kong
model of unfettered capitalism. Japan had its MITI and South Korea
closely followed the Japanese model. Singapore and Taiwan also were
much more interventionist than Hong Kong.

Still, I suspect that when the role played by industrial policy in
Japan and East Asia is better understood, its present advocates will
be less enthusiastic. Until that time, free-marketeers can take comfort from the fact that, notwithstanding Krugman's reminders of the
so-called intellectually solid cases for some government industry promotion—what he calls "strategic complementarity," statist arguments have fallen precipitously from a Myrdalian peak of massive
intervention to an obscure little corner of the universe known as
"industrial policy." If that's not progress, I don't know what is!

7

The Rise of Regionalism

Regionalism in Western Europe rose from the ashes of World War II. The economic, political, and spiritual devastation wrought by the war left Western Europe exhausted and vulnerable to a then-growing communist threat. On the theory that a rapid economic recovery was the best defense against communism, the United States put Western Europe's economic reconstruction at the very top of its postwar agenda. For this country—which emerged from the war unabashedly internationalist, anticommunist, and self-confident— the question was not whether to help Western Europe get back on its feet, but how best to proceed.

The *sine qua non* of U.S. strategy for European economic recovery was the reintegration of the Western European economies through increased intra-European trade. U.S. sponsorship of a customs union for Western Europe was motivated by this objective as was Marshall Plan aid. A customs union is a regional arrangement in which members refrain from imposing tariffs on each others' goods but levy a common tariff against nonmembers. What surer sign of U.S. self-assurance (and anticommunism) could there have been than its sponsorship of what amounted to organized discrimination against its own exports to promote European economic reconstruction?

The Customs Union Issue

As farsighted as our strategic objectives may have been toward Europe in the early postwar years, questions did arise as to whether customs union was the best means to achieve them. There was little doubt customs union would increase intra-European trade. And if the increased trade came at the expense of previously protected, high-cost member producers, European resources would be saved, and the European living standard improved, because a low-cost member source of supply substitutes for a higher-cost member source.

But what if instead of inefficient European production, the increased intra-European trade resulting from customs came at the expense of imports from efficient nonmember countries? European resources would be wasted rather than saved in this instance, because a higher-cost member source of supply substitutes for a lower-cost outsider. Clearly, a customs union would be self-defeating if it increased intra-European trade but wasted precious European resources as a result.

The possibility of this occurring was first raised in 1950 by Jacob Viner who argued that increased intra-union trade resulting from customs union could be expected to come at the expense of *both* previously protected high-cost member production *and* imports from efficient outsiders. To demonstrate his point, Viner distinguished the *trade-creation* from *trade-diversion* effects of customs union. Because customs union eliminates the protection domestic producers enjoy *vis à vis* producers of substitute goods in partner countries, it creates intra-union trade. This was well known and what most expected from customs union. But what was novel about Viner's analysis is that it demonstrated that customs union also can divert trade because it gives partner countries a tariff advantage over outsiders in member-country markets. Trade diversion takes place when the tariff advantage enjoyed by partners over outsiders is greater than the cost advantage outsiders enjoy over them. It does not take place in the opposite circumstance, notwithstanding the member's tariff advantage over outside competitors.

Trade diversion can be illustrated by a simple example. Assume that apples can be obtained at five dollars per ton on world markets but at ten dollars per ton in the partner country (the quality of apples being the same). There are no domestic apple growers in the domestic market. The cost advantage enjoyed by nonmember producers is five dollars per ton, and if there is either a tariff that is geographically nondiscriminatory or free trade before customs union, the home country imports apples from nonmembers.

Next, assume that the customs union requires the domestic country to put a six-dollars-per-ton tariff on apple imports from non-members but that apple imports from partners enter the domestic market duty-free. Thus, while the nonmember continues to enjoy a five-dollars-per-ton cost advantage by comparison with the partner country, it now suffers from a six-dollars-per-ton tariff disadvantage *vis à vis* the partner in the domestic market. Trade thus diverts from the low-cost nonmember country to the higher-cost partner country. The resource cost of trade diversion is five dollars per ton multiplied by the number of tons initially imported into the domestic country.

The world of opera provides a second, and novel, example of trade diversion. As reported by *Opera Magazine*, the Welsh National Opera tried to engage two American singers for the tenor and soprano roles in Verdi's opera *Rigoletto*. But to be able to perform in Britain, the two American singers had to receive a working permit whose application had to be supported by British Actors' Equity Association. The working permit was not required of EU artists coming to Great Britain because EU nationals are free to work in any country of the Community.

British Actors' Equity turned down the applications of the two American singers, but instead of two British artists, the Welsh Opera engaged two Italian ones. Trade diversion reduced the pleasure of the audience at the *Rigoletto* performance because the two Italians were considered less satisfactory artists than the Americans. A lower-quality source of supply had been substituted for a higher-quality one.

What factors determine whether a customs union saves or wastes resources? The height of the member country's initial tariff against partners is important. The higher the initial tariff, the greater the gains from its removal. This implies that protectionist countries stand to gain more from customs union than free traders.

A second important determinant is the height of the common external tariff. Unlike tariffs on intra-union trade, which are mandated at zero by the customs union, members have discretion over the height of the common external tariff. Other things being equal, the higher they set the common external tariff, the greater the probability the partner country's tariff advantage over outsiders will be greater than its cost disadvantage, and, thus, the greater the probability of trade diversion.

The height of the common external tariff is *the* crucial policy decision for member countries. A protectionist customs union sets its common external tariff high—a liberal one sets it low.

Viner's analysis made it clear that while customs union might improve Europe's living standard, it was not the optimal way to free up intra-European trade. For even if the customs union did save European resources, additional resources could be saved by a nondiscriminatory free trade policy (in Viner's terminology, there would be trade creation gains without trade diversion losses with global free trade). Why then did the allies opt for a regional approach to Europe's reconstruction over free trade? To answer this question, one must step outside the realm of pure economics.

The War Against Nationalism

Even before World War II had ended, the allies concluded that European nationalisms—and particularly German nationalism—had to be tempered if World War III was to be avoided. The idea was to establish regional institutions in Europe which would create and nurture a new sense of European identity to compete with Europe's long-established national identities. By far, the most important such institution was the European Economic Community (EEC), which has evolved into the European Union (EU). The Community's customs union may not have been the best way to free up intra-European trade from the purely economic point of view, but it better fit the allies' strategy of restraining European nationalisms than did universal free trade.

"The enlightened post-war agenda," writes Rudi Dornbusch, "driven by the United States but bought into vigorously by France and Germany was this: anything that would keep Germany from making war on France, dragging the whole world into these recurrent conflicts, seemed a splendid idea. And it was. The early and narrow agreements—the Marshall Plan, Coal and Steel Union, the European Payments Union—which restored regional trade all created a pattern of cooperation and regional institutions that broke the ice and set a pattern. Later, the move to a Common Market brought about a major identity boost for Europe and a growth boost at the same time. One more round, the completion of the 'integrated market' in 1992, sought to transform Europe into an integrated and competitive market of the kind the U.S. represents so strikingly."[1]

Because of its interest in diluting European nationalism, almost from its very inception the Common Market had more on its plate than mere intra-European trade liberalization. There was early talk of harmonizing member taxes, assimilating member macroeconomic policies, eliminating national currencies, establishing a European central bank, and so on. None of these regionalist schemes has yet been effectuated—nor are they likely to in the foreseeable future. The reason is simple. European nationalism has proved more resistant to regional encroachments than Community founders had anticipated.

One explanation for the resilience of European nationalism is that while regionalism has been favored by Europe's leadership elites, it has yet to take hold with Europe's masses. The recent debate over the Maastricht treaty is a case in point. The treaty, which was agreed to by EU leaders in the Dutch town of Maastricht in December 1991, lays down the strict requirements for European monetary union— budget deficits have to be below three percent of Gross Domestic Product, and the public debt to GDP ratio must be less than 60 percent. Europe's elites favor the treaty but popular opposition is so palpable that several Community members, such as Germany, Great Britain, and Italy, refused to submit it to popular referendum for fear it would be rejected. What better sign can there be that nationalism is alive and well and living in Western Europe?

One reason the masses in Europe are resistant to Europeanism is the growth of the "income transfer" state. Britons do not want their money transferred to Greeks, Germans don't want their money transferred to Brits, and so on. Indeed, in today's Europe, the "new regionalism" is less the merging of nation states into larger units than the splintering of nation states into smaller ones. Such splintering is not only for reasons of race and ethnicity as in Bosnia. The more income transfer government does, the more pressure on amalgamated political jurisdictions to separate into distinct groupings of homogeneous individuals.

The Lombards in Italy are a case in point. The burgeoning popularity of the Northern or Lombard League is primarily due to the reluctance of the Lombards to continually transfer huge sums of money to Italy's south. Alan Cowell writes in the *New York Times*:

> Initially called the Lombard League, the organization took its name directly from the league of northern cities in the twelfth and thirteenth centuries that rebelled against the Holy Roman Emperors. It's appeal reflects a longstanding complaint among northerners: with fifteen percent of the population, the industrialized, affluent Lombardy region provides twenty-five percent of the gross national product, pays twenty-five percent of the taxes but receives only

eighteen percent of the pie in state services while billions go unac-
counted for in subsidies and other payouts to the Mafia-dominated,
politically connected south. . . .

What league members say they are engaged in is a tax revolt
against a Rome-based bureaucracy whose decisions are guided by
political patronage and marked by notorious inefficiency.[2]

A second factor working against Europeanism is the expansion of
the European Union to include dramatically different nation states
with little in common except the desire not to be left out of the "new
Europe." The shifting of authority from national to regional levels
was less controversial in the early days when the Common Market
had only six members—West Germany, France, Italy, the Netherlands, Belgium, and Luxembourg. The Benelux countries always have
had strong regionalistic traditions, France wanted to use the Community to control Germany, and a defeated and divided Germany
saw regionalism as the way back to respectability and influence.

But the expansion of the so-called "inner six" to twelve, including such strongly nationalistic countries as Great Britain, clearly has
made life difficult for Europeanists. "What our readers want from
Europe," reports the *Sun* of London, "is simple: an open, free and liberal trading area within which they can create wealth and jobs, make
their own laws, retain their own culture, and run their own lives. . . .
They do not want to be dictated to by an unelected European commission, which is run by expatriate civil servants detached from
domestic reality, and backed up by an unelected, politicized European Court."[3]

A Cross of Fixed Exchange Rates

When Britain joined the Common Market, it brought not only
strongly nationalistic ideas as to how to run the Community, but an
economy with historical rates of inflation much higher than those of
Germany. This raised serious questions as to the compatibility of
Great Britain and other high-inflation new members (such as Spain
and Portugal) with the Community's long-term objective of establishing full monetary union—i.e. a single European currency and a
European central bank. Monetary union long has been a key component of the Europeanists' strategy to promote a unified Europe.

The assimilation or convergence of national macroeconomic policies required for monetary union would be a relatively simple matter
if a true Europeanist spirit existed in the Community. Divergent
countries voluntarily would adjust their national policies to the Com-

munity norm. But the evident lack of such spirit has constrained Europeanists to eschew volunteerism and instead adopt symbolism and pressure tactics to coerce a unity that doesn't exist today, and is not likely to exist in the future.

To force convergence of national macroeconomic policies, the Community established a fixed-currency-exchange-rate scheme known as the Exchange Rate Mechanism or ERM. The idea behind ERM is that its rigidly fixed exchange rates would force high inflation countries like Italy and Great Britain to adjust their macroeconomic policies to get inflation rates down to German levels. This substitution of symbolism for substance—that fixed exchange rates alone implied a unity of national macroeconomic policies—clearly was untenable. When push came to shove, it was the ERM that was abandoned, not the diversity of national policies.

The "coup de grace" for the ERM came when West German Chancellor Helmut Kohl refused to raise taxes on West Germans to finance the substantial income transfers from West to East upon German reunification. This forced the Bundesbank to pursue a high-interest-rate policy. If the non-German ERM countries had devalued their currencies against the German mark under these circumstances, the ERM might have been saved. But they did not. Instead, they raised their domestic interest rates the extent necessary to keep the parities of their currencies fixed to the German mark even though their own stagnated domestic economies could not support the high rates. The result was the worst recession Europe has experienced in several decades.

This point was made most elegantly in the *Financial Times* by six M.I.T. economists. "By far the most important factor for this debacle [rising unemployment in Europe] is the Bundesbank's policy of high interest rates, combined with certain features of the European Monetary System which have forced other countries to follow suit," write the M.I.T. "Gang of Six." "These include the mobility of capital across member countries and the fact that central banks have interpreted the rules of the exchange rate mechanism to require not only the maintenance of fixed exchange rates but also the avoidance of parity adjustments.

"The result of high interest rates across Europe has been that unemployment has risen to record levels. Governments have done little but seek a variety of excuses for the loss of jobs. It looks as if the 1930s are being re-enacted. Then, it was felt to be imperative to hang on to gold at any price: today the feeling is to hang on the D-Mark."[4]

The actual demise of the ERM began in September 1992 in an

atmosphere of intra-European rancor and acrimony. First, Great Britain was forced to withdraw in circumstances that left the British then-chancellor of the Exchequer, Norman Lamont, and the former Bundesbank president, Helmut Schlesinger, at each other's throats over whether the Bundesbank had been sufficiently supportive of the British in their failed attempt to stay in the ERM. The Italian exit—which was less acrimonious—followed the British by a few days. Next, it was the French franc's turn to come under speculative pressure. In August 1993, the Bundesbank refused to lower its domestic interest rates to support the then-beleaguered franc. The French were unable to defend their own currency because they were in a negative-net-foreign-exchange-reserve position. When the EU decided to widen the allowable bands of currency fluctuation about the targeted ERM parity from a maximum of five percent to a maximum of thirty percent, the ERM was effectively disbanded. By that decision, Europe effectively adopted a system of (dirty) floating rates (floating with occasional central bank interventions) to replace the ERM fixed-exchange-rate system. Dirty floating rates persist to this day in Europe.

The French, in particular, were extremely distressed by the breakdown of the ERM. Ex-prime minister Edouard Balladur actually went on French television to blame Anglo-Saxon currency speculators "living in London and New York" for the fall of both the franc and the ERM. Balladur's attack elicited the following response from the editors of the *Financial Times*:

> Mr. Balladur believes the security of his country has been endangered. But perhaps what has been endangered is the reputation of its policymakers. Those in office usually believe that their policies express the long-term interests of their people, while speculative attacks reveal the irresponsibility, if not wickedness, of markets. But that conclusion is not self-evident.
>
> In this case, speculators doubted the willingness of the French people to tolerate an unnecessary recession in the name of European integration. By doubting it, they created the conditions in which that policy could change, a result that seems benign.
>
> Whenever a perfectly good explanation can be found for the behaviour of individual investors, conspiracy theories are unnecessary. Currency markets are the largest and most liquid in the world. The envisaged collusion among participants is inconceivable. To argue otherwise is to indulge in paranoia.[5]

It is understandable, of course, that government officials like Balladur who had staked their political careers on rigidly fixed exchange rates and a "franc fort" (strong franc) policy would be distressed by the breakdown of the ERM. It also is understandable that the bureaucrats in Brussels—for example, former-president of the European Commission Jacques Delors—would be unhappy that their favorite vehicle for forcing European economies to converge in order to reach European Monetary Union had been sidetracked. But one wonders what could be more damaging to European unity than a premature convergence scheme like the ERM which fails in an orgy of intra-European recriminations and bad feelings. If European unity ever is to become a reality, European leaders must put such schemes on the back burner until the masses truly are ready for them.

The collapse of the ERM, though a defeat for Brussels bureaucrats, did not represent a similar setback for European integration. The *Financial Times* editors warn of the danger of identifying the ERM with European economic integration:

> Exaggerating the wisdom of governments and the follies or even wickedness of markets is, unfortunately, not the only mistake that has been made [by Mr. Balladur]. As important has been the undue identification of the cause of the European integration with a particular monetary mechanism, a mistake that parallels earlier worship of the common agricultural policy. The foundation for European integration has, in fact, been the integration of the economies of member states by the progressively increasing freedom of movement of goods, services, labour and capital. The ERM, or even economic and monetary union, can be justified largely to the extent that they support such integration.
>
> This is why talk of exchange controls is self-defeating. In the absence of some kind of global tax on foreign exchange transactions, which seems infeasible in practice and questionable in theory, the only way to try to prevent what happened to the ERM would be a return to tight national exchange controls. But this would fragment the single market for capital and severely hamper those in labour and services. Since the ERM has often been justified as the monetary counterpart of the single market, it would be perverse to adopt measures that would destroy what the mechanism is supposed to preserve.[6]

Notwithstanding the wisdom of this editorial, the *Financial Times* reported Jacques Delors, then-president of the European Commission, to be pressing for European exchange controls to fortify the ERM. "Mr. Jacques Delors ... is pressing for a monetary 'fortress Europe' to deter U.S. and other non-EC speculators from targeting currencies inside the European Monetary Systems. After days of confusion, senior EC officials have confirmed that Mr. Delors favors selective measures such as temporary capital controls on foreigners engaged in short-term speculation—such as Mr. George Soros, the New York-based investor. Mr. Delors called for collective EC action against speculators on Wednesday during a bitter and at times emotional speech to the European parliament in Strasbourg, in which he attacked 'Anglo-Saxon' critics of European Monetary Union and branded currency speculators as 'golden boys'. Many interpreted Mr. Delors' remarks as advocating at least partial re-imposition of capital controls."[7]

Clearly, the European Commission has lost its bearings when its president publicly declares that fixed exchange rates are more important for Europe than the free movement of capital between member states.

Delors's call for capital controls to defend currency exchange rates, however, comes as no surprise to ERM critics who have based their opposition to fixed rates precisely on the grounds that fixed rates would spawn interventions in international trade and capital flows to defend the fixed rate. The idea that fixed currency exchange rates, or common currency, are necessary conditions for the proper functioning of economic integration is nonsense. Though the opposite also is not the case—that flexible exchange rates (floating without central bank intervention) are a necessary condition—it *is* true that flexible rates are a better guarantor than fixed rates that the basic fabric of economic integration—the free movement of goods and factor resources—will be preserved in the face of economic disturbances in a single member country or set of countries.

The "dirty float" emanating from the August 1993 breakdown of the ERM thus not only failed to threaten the basics of Europe's integration, but actually supported them. To preserve the ERM under market conditions prevailing at that time clearly would have required France to impose capital controls, because the selling of the French franc by currency speculators simply had become too intense for French interest rate hikes to quell.

The Drive for Common Money

The prime force behind the myth that a diverse Europe is incompatible with an integrated Europe are Brussels bureaucrats whose personal power, prestige, and influence depend upon their ability to build up centralized government in Brussels at the expense of member states. The European Commission promotes "convergence," the "harmonization of national policies," and "political solidarity" not because European economic integration requires any of these things. Rather it is because the Europeanists in Brussels require them to further their own exaggerated ambitions and big-government agenda. European economic integration, for example, doesn't need common money and the European Monetary Union to be successful. The Commission wants it to force centralization of European monetary authority.

Common money, however, has more backers in Europe than just the Brussels Commission. Helmut Kohl is the most powerful politician in Europe today, and he wants common money to further the postwar German strategy of using European regionalism to dampen fears of resurgent German nationalism (particularly in light of German reunification). Indeed, it is because of German sponsorship that common money has come to mean hard money in Europe. Kohl realizes that the German people are not likely to sacrifice the "hard" Deutsche Mark for the "soft" Euro (as the proposed common currency is called). France and the other EMU participants will have to demonstrate to German satisfaction their monetary predispositions are as anti-inflationary and hard money as the Germans'. The crucial test is Maastricht—to participate in the EMU, budget deficits for all participants must be below three percent of GDP, and the public debt ratio must be less than 60 percent of GDP.

At a time when all prospective EMU members—including Germany—have budget deficits well in excess of the three percent target, it is clear that the adjustment to EMU will be extremely deflationary at a time when most of Europe has high unemployment. Rudi Dornbusch writes: "There is virtually no country with a budget that makes the Maastricht criteria, including Germany and France, the two key countries. As a result, all of Europe is plunging into budget cutting, all at once, with the likely outcome of a slowdown. True, the budget cuts are appropriate even without EMU, but their timing, size and coincidence will cut into growth, raise unemployment further, add to the costs of EMU before it starts. Monetary authorities have shown no disposition to accommodate. They have their own agenda: hold tight to the last moment, help shape the right attitude for the new Central Bank. The combination of overly tight monetary policy and determined budget cutting suggest a tough time ahead for Europe."[8]

The realization that EMU promises profound changes in the European lifestyle has prompted an unlikely political alliance between left-wing social democrats and right-wing nationalists to defeat common money—at least, the hard EMU variety.

"As the 1997 deadline for deciding who will join EMU draws

near, many Europeans are realizing that a single currency involves more than simply switching from marks or francs or gilders into Euro, the name chosen for the common currency," reports the *Wall Street Journal*. "By imposing strict budgetary, debt and inflation ceilings on member states, EMU would radically change Europe's way of life. It would force an overhaul of what Mr. Chirac (current President of France) calls 'the European social model'—a mixture of generous welfare spending, protective labor legislation and a strong government role as employer, shareholder, regulator and provider of 'public services' ranging from telecommunications to health and education.

"All over Europe, the austerity policies that underpin the single currency are coming under fire. In Germany's biggest postwar demonstration, 350,000 people recently marched in Bonn to protest social spending cutbacks. In France, which endured three weeks of crippling strikes in December, unions are calling for walkouts this fall to protest public-sector job cuts. In Spain, unions are calling for a general strike against government plans to privatize an array of state companies. In Italy, union protests forced the government to soften its tough stand on public-sector wages."[9]

The biggest threat to Europe's welfare state comes not from foreign trade and international competition, but from European monetary union and the hard Euro.

Customs Union Is Not Enough

The European Union's most notable achievement in its almost four decades of existence has been its customs union. But while the customs union—which has been shown to be trade-creating—has been good as far as it goes, it hasn't gone nearly far enough. The customs union does not cover domestic subsidies and import quotas. The trend of substituting subsidies for tariffs as protectionist devices has made the elimination of customs duties on intra-European trade increasingly irrelevant. The union's common external tariff does not imply a common trade policy because it excludes import quotas. What good is a low common external tariff if it is offset by restrictive import quotas on nonmember imports?

Perhaps the most important deficiency of the EU customs union, however, is that it does not cover agricultural trade. Trade in agricultural products takes place according to the EU's so-called Common Agricultural Policy (CAP). The CAP calls for a common internal EU price for agricultural goods—a price fixed not by the most efficient producer in the Community market as a result of free competition, but by the Eurocrats in Brussels at a level that allows even the least efficient Community producer to stay in business. To support a higher internal than world price level, the EU tariffs imports and subsidizes exports of agricultural products.

If the EC market was a small market, the tariffs and export subsidies needed to support high EC prices would have little effect on agricultural prices *in world markets*. But the EC market is huge. Accordingly, the excess supply created by the EU tariffs and export subsidies lowers world price, causing damage to foreign sellers of agricultural goods. This has put the United States, the Third World, and Eastern Europe on the same side of a major trade issue. All three are agricultural exporters and all three are being damaged by the CAP.

Eastern Europe is of particular concern. How ironic—and outrageous—that as the Iron Curtain has come down, it has been replaced by a butter curtain, a wheat curtain and a corn curtain. "The new democracies of Eastern Europe complain bitterly that the EC is hampering their path to post-Communist prosperity by blocking the entry of many of their products," reports the *Wall Street Journal*.[10] The editors of the *Financial Times* argue that the EC "must review its reform of the common agricultural policy, largely to increase opportunities for eastern European agriculture."[11] And Lionel Barber writes in the *International Economy*: "The lack of [European] leadership has created a policy toward the former communist countries which is self-centered, short-sighted and downright dangerous. . . . A new Iron Curtain has descended upon the middle of Europe, dividing rich Western capitalist countries from their poor ex-communist cousins in the East."[12]

The Common Agricultural Policy may be the most egregious example of EU bias against Eastern European exports, but it's not the only one. There is the customs union, of course, whose common external tariff discriminates against Eastern European nonagricultural exports. And the persistent attempts at European Monetary Union (EMU) have reduced Eastern exports into the West because of its contractionary bias. There is no theoretical reason why EMU should have a contractionary bias, but that is the way it has been working out in practice. Pegging their currencies to the Deutsche Mark has meant abnormally high interest rates outside Germany (particularly in France). And the additional requirement for monetary union set out in the Maastricht treaty, that members reduce their fiscal deficits to three percent of the gross domestic product, adds to EMU contractionary pressures. The result of artificially high interest rates and fiscal contraction has been high unemployment and sluggish economies which, through income effects, reduce East European exports to the EU.

An American Answer to Europe

A fundamental law of customs unions is that once the union is established with important trading countries as members, there is inexorable pressure for the union to expand. The reason for this is simple to understand: countries outside the customs unions need to join, because they would rather be helped than burdened by the common external tariff.

In Europe, the European Union originally consisted of six countries—West Germany, France, Italy, Belgium, the Netherlands, and Luxembourg. Today, it consists of twelve—Ireland, Denmark, Spain, Portugal, Greece, and the United Kingdom have been added—and the expansion process is not complete. With the end of the Cold War, the so-called neutral countries—Sweden, Finland, and Austria—have joined, and several Eastern European countries are anxious to follow suit. Only proud Norway has rejected EU membership.

Not all nations, of course, can circumvent Europe's trade diversion by joining the Union. The nations of North America are obvious victims of European trade discrimination. Yet they cannot join the European Union by virtue of their geographic locale. NAFTA or the North American Free Trade Area is this continent's answer to the European Union.

NAFTA is a free-trade area, not a customs union. A customs union has a common external tariff. A free-trade area allows individual members to levy their own different tariff rates on imports from nonmembers. Both, however, remove tariffs on trade between member countries. A free trade area requires "rules of origin" (controls) at the common border to insure the low-tariff country does not become the de-facto common external tariff for the entire free-trade area.

The reason NAFTA adopted the free-trade area rather than the customs-union form of regional trade liberalization was to avoid the political difficulties and supra-nationalistic implications of forging a common external tariff. Unlike the EU, NAFTA's agenda begins and ends with regional free trade. It has no interest in promoting political unity—nor does it seek regional monetary union, fiscal harmonization, harmonization of social policies, and so on. European-style supra-nationalistic institutions—a "North American" Commission, for example—are not in the cards even as discussion points.

The concepts of trade creation and trade diversion—used to analyze customs unions—can be applied to the analysis of free-trade areas as well. Because of the removal of intra-area tariffs, NAFTA can be expected to increase trade between the United States, Mexico, and Canada. The key question for efficient resource allocation is whether the increased intra-area trade comes at the expense of protected production in member countries (trade creation) or existing imports from nonmembers (trade diversion).

If the increased intra-union trade comes at the expense of previously protected, high-cost member production, member resources are saved, and NAFTA increases the area's living standard. On the other hand, if the increased trade between the three members comes at the expense of their preexisting trade with nonmember countries (Japan, for example), NAFTA wastes North American resources. The evidence strongly suggests that NAFTA will be *net* trade creating, which is why the vast majority of economists in this country support the treaty. North American countries trade more with one another than with outsiders—implying minimal trade diversion—while each member protects a substantial amount of local production from competition with other members—implying substantial trade-creation opportunities.

What has been the result of NAFTA so far? One year after the treaty was signed, *Business Week* reported that trade between the NAFTA countries expanded substantially: "Trucks are rumbling back and forth across the U.S.-Mexico border, carrying tomatoes, chewing gum, Ford Broncos, electric generators, and Maybelline mascara at a feverish clip. U.S. and Canadian companies are rushing to set up offices and factories in Nuevo Laredo, Monterrey, and Guadalajara.

"In the north, Canada's Bank of Montreal has just launched the first mutual fund, to be marketed in all three countries, targeting companies poised to cash in on the North American Free Trade Agreement. The portfolio includes key players in Mexico's construction craze: Quebec's Bombardier, telecommunications giant Telefonos de Mexico, and Caterpillar.

"As the first anniversary of NAFTA's signing approaches, the treaty is doing what it was designed to do: erase national borders for business and create a new North American Market. As cross-border commerce quickens its pace under the accord, executives are no longer planning operations just in the U.S., Canada, or Mexico. They're thinking North America. While NAFTA hasn't yet created all the jobs or given Mexico the boost its most zealous backers predicted, it is paying big dividends in increased trade."[13]

Business Week's evaluation was made before Mexico's financial crisis and peso devaluation. Though the crisis has not fully played itself out at the time of this writing, certain things are clear. Mexico's economy is going to experience a considerable recession whatever happens—and this will cut into Mexican imports especially of consumer goods. In fact, in 1995 consumer imports did fall substantially though Mexican imports of intermediate goods increased. The reason for the increase is that Mexican exports to the United States boomed in 1995, and these exports used the imported intermediate goods as inputs in their production processes. According to Mexican Finance Minister Guillermo Ortiz, NAFTA and has been critical for Mexico's 1995 export boom. If there had been no NAFTA, there would have been no export boom, and the economic and political crisis in Mexico would have been far more serious than it in fact has been. This would have been bad not only for Mexico but for the United States as well.

Wage Convergence in NAFTA: How NAFTA Helps Solve the U.S.-Mexican Migration Problem

While NAFTA can be expected to save U.S. resources, it may not benefit each and every group in the community. One U.S. group likely to lose from the trade agreement is unskilled labor. Because the United States is a high-skill-abundant, low-skill-scarce economy by comparison with Mexico, the expected reallocation of labor induced by NAFTA will be from low-skill-intensive to high-skill-intensive industries. This means unskilled labor will be released from contracting industries at a faster pace than it will be absorbed by expanding industries in the United States. The resultant unemployment of unskilled workers can be mitigated only if their wages are reduced.

NAFTA's downward pressure on the wages of unskilled workers in the United States, however, does not mean there will be downward wage pressure throughout the entire free trade area. On the contrary, because NAFTA implies a reallocation of resources from high-skill- to low-skill-intensive industries in Mexico, the wages of unskilled workers in Mexico will be bid up. Low-skill wages rise in Mexico, and fall in the United States, because free trade encourages each country to economize on its scarce factor of production. Free trade implies less demand for U.S. low-skill labor—our relatively scarce factor—and more demand for Mexico's low-skill workers—

Mexico's relatively abundant factor. One result of NAFTA therefore will be a tendency towards a convergence of the wages of unskilled workers in Mexico and the United States.

Wage conversion between Mexico and the United States will tend to reduce the flow of Mexican workers to the United States. More opportunity for low-skill workers in Mexico, combined with less opportunity in the United States, will conspire to accomplish what barbed-wire barricades erected at the common border cannot— a natural alleviation of Mexican migration to the United States without the use of force, bloodshed, or excessive discord between the two countries. NAFTA will make nativist legislation like California's Proposition 187 and the barbed-wire policies of Pat Buchanan irrelevant, because *voluntarily* fewer and fewer illegal migrants will seek to enter this country. Economics teaches us that commodity trade and labor mobility are substitutes for one another. The more a given amount of international exchange takes the form of commodity trade, the less labor movement there will be.

AFTA After NAFTA

For the same reason that Europe's Common Market is expanding, NAFTA can be expected to add to its original membership in future years. No Western Hemispheric country will want its goods discriminated against in the North American market, particularly those in South and Central America, such as Chile, Argentina, Venezuela, and the Caribbean nations, that do substantial business in North America. These nations will seek to join NAFTA and in all likelihood be accepted, first, because it will be politically difficult for the United States to shut these countries out of the trade group (e.g., African-Americans are said to be particularly keen to have the Caribbean nations in NAFTA. It is only a matter of time before Hispanic Americans will demand other Hispanic nations be included as well.)[14] Second, if we do try to exclude these nations, they will form their own regional blocs that discriminate against U.S. exports.

AFTA—an "Americas Free Trade Area"—is certain to evolve out of the present NAFTA. "With approval of the North American Free Trade Agreement, leaders of virtually every major Latin American nation except Brazil said their country should be next in line to join the North American trade bloc," writes James Brooke in the *New York Times*. "'The free-trade agreements have developed beyond all expectations,' said Noemi Sanin, Foreign Minister of Colombia, a nation that is negotiating trade accords with 22 other Latin American countries. 'Before the end of the century, we aspire to achieve the planet's most important trading bloc—the American bloc.'"[15]

From the viewpoint of efficient resource allocation, AFTA's effects should be similar to NAFTA's—only more so. Trade diversion will be minimal because the nations of North, South, and Central America trade more with one another than with outsiders. Trade creation will be substantial because, notwithstanding high current levels of intra-area trade, local producers continue to receive significant protection in certain industries.

Moreover, AFTA can play a significant role in neutralizing European protectionism. The fact that AFTA will be able to divert member imports from European markets gives the Europeans an incentive to impose reasonable tariffs against Western Hemisphere exports. Otherwise, they could find themselves excluded from the huge Western Hemispheric market. Similarly, because the European Union can divert member imports from North, South, and Central America gives the Americas an incentive to be reasonable in their own trade policies.

The situation is analogous to that which prevailed in the national security arena under the doctrine of Mutual Assured Destruction. MAD, as it was known, helped prevent nuclear war throughout the Cold War period. The Soviet Union dared not launch a nuclear first strike against the West because it knew the United States could reciprocate in kind. And the United States similarly demurred from a nuclear first strike against the Soviet Union because it knew the Soviets also could strike back with nuclear weapons.

A world of regional trading blocs need not be a protectionist world—it could be an important stopping off point on the road to global free trade.

One final reason AFTA would be a positive development for the world economy is that it would encourage the nations of the Western Hemisphere to adopt market-oriented economic reforms. Indeed, the mere prospect of admission to the free-trade bloc already has encouraged several Latin American countries to alter their economic policies from statism to the free market. "Taking North America's free-trade gospel to heart, Latin American nations are bulldozing tariff barriers with such energy that economists in the region predict that most trade within Latin America will be duty-free by the end of the decade," writes James Brooke in the *New York Times*. "Many Latin American leaders, recalling President Bush's conception of a trade zone stretching from Alaska to Argentina, say that today's free market-directed policies are preparing their economies for a day when the North American trade zone expands South."[16]

"In 1990," reports Carla Ann Robbins in the *Wall Street Journal*, "when President Bush proposed making NAFTA a hemisphere-wide free-trade zone, Latin American governments took him at his word. They tore down trade barriers and introduced internal economic reforms, in hopes of speeding their admission to the free-trade club. . . . The promise of NAFTA didn't begin the trend toward market liberalization in Latin America, but it did reinforce and deepen the process, analysts say."[17]

Odd Men Out

The rise of regionalism in Europe and the Western Hemisphere threatens to leave Japan and East Asia the odd men out. Unable to join either Europe or America by virtue of its geographic locale, Japan also is unable to form a free trade area of its own in the Pacific Basin for want of willing partners. China is the most logical partner, but is years, maybe decades, away from such an arrangement. The South Koreans want no part of a partnership with Japan.

Still Japan and countries like South Korea do have various options open to combat foreign-trade diversion. Primary amongst these is using foreign investment to ferret under foreign-trade barriers. When Japan or South Korea builds an automobile factory in the United States, for example, it becomes a NAFTA insider—the beneficiary rather than victim of trade discrimination. Similarly, Japan and South Korea become European Union insiders when they build plants in the European Union.

The question arises: what effect does such Japanese foreign investment in Europe and America—to circumvent regional trade barriers against outsiders—have on efficiency in the allocation of the world's resources? The answer depends upon whether or not Japan's cost advantage at home can be transferred to the foreign country in which Japan invests.

If, for example, a plant manufacturing Honda cars is transferred to the United States and the U.S. plant is as efficient as the Honda plant in Japan, then NAFTA's trade diversion effect is neutralized or offset by the Japanese foreign investment. U.S. consumption of Honda cars continues at the same low-resource cost even though the geographical site of production has been moved. On the other hand, if the Honda plant in the United States is less efficient than the Honda plant in Japan, the Japanese investment has no effect on NAFTA's diversion of resources from a low-cost to high-cost source of supply. U.S. consumers continue to consume Honda cars but NAFTA increases the resource cost of this consumption because Hondas made in the United States cost more resources than Hondas made in Japan.

The effect of ferret-style Japanese investment in free-trade areas and customs unions from which Japan is excluded is a priori indeterminate—it may offset the bloc's trade diversion effect but it need not do so.

A second mechanism Japan can use to defend itself from foreign regional trade blocs is capital investment in less-developed countries (LDCs). Such investment can lower the cost of producing Japanese goods below what would obtain in Japan itself, helping Japan overcome the trade discrimination it faces in foreign markets. The effect European and American regional trade blocs have in "pushing" Japanese production out of Japan into the hinterland is extremely positive for at least three reasons. First, it brings needed economic activity to the less developed countries. Second, it alleviates Japan's severe environmental problems. And, most important, it benefits consumers of Japanese goods throughout the world.

How fortunate that Japan has sufficient trade surpluses to finance its capital investment in the LDCs! Otherwise, Japan's likely reaction to Western trade discrimination could well be increased Japanese protectionism. Bill Clinton and Mickey Kantor, are you taking notes?

Notes

Introduction

1. Walter H. Heller, "Fiscal Policies for Underdeveloped Countries," in Richard Bird and Oliver Oldman, eds., Readings on Taxation in Developing Countries (Baltimore: The John Hopkins Press, 1964), 5.
2. Martin Wolf, *Financial Times* (Oct. 7, 1994).
3. Lionel Barber, "The New Hypocrites," *The International Economy* (September/October 1993).

Chapter 1

1. Bob Davis, "In Debate over NAFTA, Many See Global Trade As Symbol of Hardship," the *Wall Street Journal* (Oct. 20, 1993).
2. Peter Passell, "How Free Trade Prompts Growth: A Primer," *New York Times* (Dec. 15, 1993).
3. Paul A. Samuelson and William D. Nordhaus, *Economics Twelfth Edition*, (New York: McGraw-Hill, 1985), 834–35.
4. Russell D. Roberts calls the theory of comparative advantage the "roundabout way to wealth" in his insightful fable of free trade and protectionism. See Russell D. Roberts, *The Choice* (Prentice Hall, 1994).
5. Robert Reich, "Trade With Mexico Is a Boon for U.S. Workers," *Wall Street Journal* (April 30, 1993).
6. Passell, 1993.
7. Lionel Barber, "The New Hypocrites," *The International Economy* (Sept./Oct. 1993).
8. Karen Elliott House, "Japan's Decline, America's Rise," *Wall Street Journal* (April 21, 1992).

Chapter 2

1. Gwen Ifill, "Clinton and the Japanese Premier Scold Each Other on Trade Issues," *New York Times* (April 17, 1993).
2. Peter Passell, "Big Trade Deficit with Japan: Some Think It's No Problem," *New York Times* (Feb. 15, 1994).
3. Editorial on "Trade Sanity With Japan," *New York Times* (June 16, 1993).
4. Michael Prowse, "A Prussian in the White House," *Financial Times* (Feb. 21, 1994): 14.
5. "US Economists Attack 'Myopic' Trade Calls," *Financial Times* (Oct. 7, 1993).
6. Robert Novak, "Truth or Trade: Clinton Blinked," *Chicago Sun-Times* (July 3, 1995).

Chapter 3

1. Milton and Rose Friedman, *Free to Choose: A Personal Statement.* (New York: Harcourt Brace & Company, 1980), 50. See also, James Bovard, *The Fair Trade Fraud* (New York: St. Martin's Press, 1991).
2. Milton Friedman, "In Defense of Dumping," *Commonwealth* (Aug 24, 1987).
3. Friedman, 1987.
4. J. Michael Finger, *Antidumping: How it Works and Who Gets Hurt* (Ann Arbor: The University of Michigan Press, 1993).
5. James Bovard, "Commerce's Latest Fair Trade Fraud," *Wall Street Journal* (Jan. 28, 1993).
6. James Bovard, "Steel Rulings Dump on America," *Wall Street Journal* (June 23, 1993).
7. Wolfgang Munchau, "Wage Dumping Irks German Jobless," *Financial Times* (March 30/31, 1996).
8. Munchau, 1996.
9. Editorial, *New York Times* (Dec. 24, 1994).
10. Nancy Dunne, "Steel Users Condemn U.S. Trade Cases," *Financial Times* (June 7, 1993).
11. "The 'Plain Folks' Kantor Risks Alienating," *Financial Times* (May 11, 1993).
12. *Financial Times*, 1993.
13. David E. Sanger, "I.B.M. Chief Issues Threat on U.S. Tariff," *New York Times* (Nov. 8, 1991).
14. Paul Magnusson, "Did Washington Lose Sight of the Big Picture?," *Business Week* (Dec. 2, 1991).
15. Eric J. Savitz, "Dangerous Display," *Barron's Magazine* (June 28, 1993); author's underlining.
    Alas, the recision of the 63 percent tariff by the Clinton Administration has not meant a corresponding recision of protection of the U.S. flat-panel screen industry. For Clinton replaced the ill-advised tariff with equally ill-advised direct budgetary subsidies. "The White House has approved a proposal to invest $1 billion to assist U.S. companies to manufacture the flat panel displays used

in computers, portable electronic devices, and critical military equipment,"
writes Keith Bradsher in the *New York Times*. "The proposal will give matching
fund grants to U.S. companies that invest in display research and production.
U.S. companies have less than 3 percent of the global market of flat panel displays, while Japanese companies such as Sharpe Corp. own the rest. The administration's plan is to bypass economic forces by subsidizing the development
effort. Department of Defense officials believe producing displays in the U.S. is
important because Japanese firms are reluctant to sell them devices for its
weapon systems, and a lack of supply could curtail development in other U.S.
industries such as computers and telecommunications." [Keith Bradsher, "U.S.
to Aid Industry in Computer Battle with Japanese," *New York Times* (April 27,
1994)].

Though the rationale for the Clinton administration's first major foray into a
national industrial policy was alleged to be military—that Japan's Sharpe Corporation refused to sell flat screens to the U.S. military—its true purpose was protectionist. "The flat-panel program goes well beyond the military," writes the
Wall Street Journal. "Clintonites are trying to put together a model of technolog-
ical development that will equip U.S. companies to break into markets already
seized by Japanese concerns. If the plan succeeds, the Clinton administration
could apply the lessons to technologies such as electronic packaging, robotics,
ceramics, and precision machinery, where Japanese firms have big leads." [Bob
Davis and G. Pascal Zachary, "Politics and Policy: Electronics Firms Get Push
From Clinton To Join Industrial Policy Initiative in Flat-Panel Displays," *Wall
Street Journal* (April 28, 1994).]

16. Milton and Rose Friedman, *Free To Choose: A Personal Statement* (New York:
Harcourt Brace & Company, 1980).
17. L. William Seidman, "Block the Bailout: Let Market Solve Mexico's Woes," *Wall
Street Journal* (Jan. 23, 1995).

Chapter 4

1. See Melvyn Krauss, "The Swedish Tax Revolt," *The Wall Street Journal* (Feb. 1,
1978).
2. Roger Cohen, "European Community Backs Plan to Create Jobs by Reducing
Costs," *New York Times* (Dec. 11, 1993).
3. Edmund S. Phelps, "Summiteers: Your Taxes Kill Jobs," *Wall Street Journal*
(March 14, 1994).
4. Alberto Alesina and Roberto Perotti, "The Welfare State and Competitiveness,"
National Bureau of Economic Research, Working Paper No. 4810.
5. Andrew Gowers and David Buchan, "EU Action on Unfair Trade Urged by Balladur," *Financial Times* (Dec. 31, 1993).
6. "The Global Economy," *The Economist* (Oct. 1, 1994).
7. Asra Nomani, "In Vote's Wake, an Odd Coalition of Opponents Sharpens
Swords that May Clash on Priorities," *Wall Street Journal* (Nov. 19, 1993).
8. *Wall Street Journal* (Dec. 10, 1993).

9. Ralph Nader, "WTO Means Rule by Unaccountable Tribunals," *Wall Street Journal* (Aug. 17, 1994).

10. Melvyn Krauss, *The New Protectionism* (New York: New York University Press, 1978), 60.

11. Nader, (1994).

12. Editorial, *New York Times* (Jan. 21, 1996).

13. James Bennet, "Buchanan Dumps a Winning Stump Character Before It Could Bite," *New York Times* (March 23, 1996).

14. *New York Times* (Aug. 1, 1994).

15. Editorial, *New York Times* (July 23, 1994); author's underlining.

16. Edmund G. Brown, Jr., "Free Trade's Huge Costs," *New York Times* (May 2, 1993).

17. Editorial, *The Financial Times* (Jan. 14, l994).

18. Graham Fraser, "PM Defends Trade Accord During Impromptu Debate, Declares Social Programs Safe," *Globe and Mail* (Nov. 3, 1988).

19. Ross Howard, "NDP Fears Future Pressure More Than Terms of Deal," *Globe and Mail* (Nov. 4, 1988).

20. This analysis is based on reasoning developed by Harry G. Johnson and myself in H.G. Johnson and M.B. Krauss, "Border Taxes, Border Tax Adjustments, Comparative Advantage and the Balance of Payments," *Canadian Journal of Economics* (Nov. 1970).

21. Rudi Dornbusch, "World Economic Trends," (July/Aug. 1996).

22. Thomas Kamm and Cacilie Rohwedder, "Many Europeans Fear Cuts in Social Benefits in One-Currency Plan," *Wall Street Journal* (July 30, 1996).

23. Anna Quindlen, "Out of the Hands of Babes," *The New York Times* (Nov, 23, 1994).

24. Quindlen, 1994.

25. Bob Herbert, "Terror in Toyland," *The New York Times* (Dec. 21, 1994).

26. Herbert, 1994.

27. Quindlen, 1994.

28. Lucy Martinez-Mont, "Sweatshops are Better Than No Shops," *Wall Street Journal* (June 25, 1996).

29. David E. Sanger, "Trade Agreement Ends Long Debate, But Not Conflicts," *New York Times* (Dec. 4, 1994).

30. Sanger, 1994.

31. Thomas L. Friedman, "Battle of the Briefcase," *New York Times* (Feb. 12, 1995).

32. Editorial, "The Morality of Animal Rights," *Financial Times* (Jan. 30, 1995).

33. *Financial Times*, 1995.

34. *Financial Times*, 1995.

35. "France to push workers' rights in WTO," Guy de Jonquieres and Robert Taylor, *Financial Times* (Feb. 2, 1995).

36. *Financial Times*, 1995.

37. Clyde H. Farnsworth, "Canada Links Trade Pact to an Accord on Subsidies," *New York Times* (Nov. 9, 1993).

38. Paul Gigot, "Kemp, Bennett Commit Grievous Act of Loyalty," *Wall Street Journal* (Oct. 28, 1994).

39. Ron Unz, *Policy Review*, (Spring 1996).
40. Paul Gigot, "Uncle Sam Wants Your Papers, Please," *Wall Street Journal* (Sept. 29, 1995).

Chapter 5

1. Barry Newman, "Bangladesh Provides Plenty of Ammunition for Critics of Food Aid," *Wall Street Journal* (April 16, 1981); author's underlining.
2. Doug Bandow and Ian Vasquez, eds., *Perpetuating Poverty* (Washington, D.C : CATO Institute, 1994), 8.
3. Bandow and Vasquez (1994), 8.
4. Rudi Dornbusch, *World Economic Trends* 1 (1995).
5. Editorial, *Financial Times* (Feb. 8, 1995).
6. L. Dudley and R.J. Sandilands, "The Side Effects of Foreign Aid: The Case of PL 480 in Colombia," Economic Development and Cultural Change 23 (Jan., 1975).
7. Peter Gumbel and Charles Goldsmith, "EC's Growing Unemployment Provokes Questions About Economic Practices," *Wall Street Journal* (June 18, 1993).
8. J. Michael Finger, "The High Cost of Trade Protectionism in the Third World," in *Perpetuating Poverty* (Washington, D.C.: Cato Institute, 1994).
9. Melanie Tammen, "Fostering Aid Addiction in Eastern Europe," *Perpetuating Poverty* (Washington, D.C.: Cato Institute, 1994), 122–123.
10. Alvin Rabushka, "Hands Out For a Handout," *Foreign Operations, Export Financing, and Related Programs Appropriations for 1993, Part 3* (1992).
11. The Congress of the United States Congressional Budget Office, *Enhancing U.S. Security Through Foreign Aid*, A CBO Study (April 1994).
12. Ibid.
13. Gottfried Haberler, "Liberal and Illiberal Development Policy: Free Trade Like Honesty is Still the Best Policy," *The World Bank Pioneer Series* (Washington, D.C.: The World Bank, 1986).
14. P.T. Bauer, *Reality and Rhetoric: Studies in the Economics of Development* (Cambridge, Mass.: Harvard University Press, 1984), 49.
15. The Congress of the United States Congressional Budget Office, *Enhancing U.S. Security Through Foreign Aid*, A CBO Study (April 1994).
16. Boris Fyodorov, "Moscow Without Mirrors," *New York Times* (April 1, 1994); author's underlining.
17. The Congress of the United States Congressional Budget Office, *Enhancing U.S. Security Through Foreign Aid*, A CBO Study (April 1994).
18. Melvyn Krauss, *How Nato Weakens The West* (New York: Simon and Schuster, 1986), 223–24.
19. Editorial, *New York Times* (July 5, 1993); author's underlining.
20. Steven Erlanger, "Russia in a Budget Fight While It Seeks Loans," *New York Times* (Oct. 24, 1994).
21. Jeff Gerth and Eliane Sciolino, "I.M.F. Head: He Speaks, and Money Talks," *New York Times* (April 2, 1996).
22. Gerth and Sciolino, 1996.

23. Alejandro J. Sucre, "Mexicans Beware! What IMF Austerity Did for Venezuelans," *Wall Street Journal* (Feb. 24, 1995).

24. Sucre, 1995.

25. Sucre, 1995.

26. Howard W. French, "Donors of Foreign Aid Have Second Thoughts," *New York Times* (April 7, 1996).

27. French, 1996.

28. Gary Hufbauer, "The Futility of Sanctions," *Wall Street Journal* (June 1, 1994).

29. Hufbauer, 1994.

30. Hufbauer, 1994.

31. Gary Clyde Hufbauer, Jeffrey J. Schott and Kimberly Ann Elliott, *Economic Sanctions Reconsidered* (Washington, D.C.: Institute for International Economics, 1990).

32. Hufbauer, 1994.

33. Howard W. French, "Despite Embargo, Haiti's Rich Seem to Get Richer," *New York Times* (May 25, 1994).

34. Roger Thurow, "Embargo Busting: Serb Economy Stays Afloat With the Help Of Criminal Network," *Wall Street Journal* (June 7, 1994); author's underlining.

35. See Anthony Lewis, "Help From Outside," *New York Times* (May 6, 1994).

36. Herman Nickel, Letters to the Editor, "South Africa Sanctions Didn't Undo Apartheid," *New York Times* (May 15, 1994).

37. Clyde H. Farnsworth, "Canada Links Trade Pact to an Accord on Subsidies."

38. Herman Nichel, Letters to the Editor, "South Africa Sanctions Didn't Undo Apartheid," *New York Times* (May 15, 1994).

39. Jerry Gray, "Foreign Investors in Libya and Iran Facing Sanctions," *New York Times* (July 24, 1996).

Chapter 6

1. Walter H. Heller, "Fiscal Policies for Underdeveloped Countries," in Richard Bird and Oliver Oldman, *Readings on Taxation in Developing Countries* (Baltimore: The Johns Hopkins Press, 1964), 5.

2. Norman S. Buchanan, "Deliberate Industrialization for Higher Incomes," *Economic Journal*, (Dec. 1946), 552.

3. Gunnar Myrdal, *An International Economy* (New York: Harper & Brothers Publishers, 1956), 201.

4. Martin Wolf, *Financial Times* (Oct. 7, 1994).

5. Richard A. Musgrave and Peggy Musgrave, *Public Finance in Theory and Practice* (New York: McGraw-Hill, 1973), 725.

6. Walter H. Heller, "Fiscal Policies for Underdeveloped Countries," in Richard Bird and Oliver Oldman, *Readings on Taxation in Developing Countries* (Baltimore: The Johns Hopkins Press, 1964), 6–7.

7. Albert O. Hirschman, *The Strategy of Economic Development* (New Haven: Yale University Press, 1958), 94.

8. Hirschman, 1958, 94.

9. Hirschman 1958, 95.

10. P.T. Bauer, *Dissent on Development* (London: Weidenfeld and Nicolson, 1971), 111.

11. Myrdal, 1956, 180.

12. Bauer, 1971, 470.

13. Bauer, 1971, 461.

14. Thomas Sowell, *Race and Culture* (New York: Harper Collins Publishers, 1994), 17–18.

15. Walter H. Heller, "Fiscal Policies for Underdeveloped Countries," in Richard Bird and Oliver Oldman, *Readings on Taxation in Developing Countries* (Baltimore: The Johns Hopkins Press, 1964), 21.

16. Myrdal, 1950, 187.

17. Myrdal, 1956, 181.

18. Robert J. Barro, "Party policies of growth," *Financial Times* (Nov. 1, 1994).

19. Dwight Perkins, "Completing China's Move to the Market," *Journal of Economic Perspectives* (Spring 1994), 29.

20. Myrdal, 1956, 222.

21. Myrdal, 1956, 276.

22. Myrdal, 1956, 279.

23. Paul Krugman, "Towards a Counter-Counter-Revolution in Development Theory," (Washington, D.C.: World Bank's *Annual Conference on Development Economics*, April 10 & May 1, 1994).

24. Ross Levine and David Renelt, "A Sensitivity Analysis of Cross-Country Growth Regressions," *American Economic Review* (Sept. 1992), 942.

25. Robert J. Barro, "Democracy: A Receipt for Growth?" *Wall Street Journal* (Dec. 1, 1994).

26. Barro, 1994.

27. Barro, 1994.

28. Krugman, 1994, 17–18.

29. Krugman, 1994, 17–18.

30. Krugman, 1994, 21.

Chapter 7

1. Rudi Dornbusch, "World Economic Trends," July/Aug. 1996, privately published by Professor Dornbusch.

2. Alan Cowell, "Italian Party Feeds on Others' Shame," *New York Times* (April 5, 1993).

3. Kevin MacKenzie, "Mass Trick Treaty," *Financial Times* (June 1, 1993).

4. Olivier Blanchard, Rudiger Dornbusch, Stanley Fischer, Franco Modigliani, Paul A. Samuelson, Robert Solow, "Why the EMS Deserves an Early Burial," *Financial Times* (July 29, 1993).

5. Editorial, "Speculators as the Scapegoats," *Financial Times* (Aug. 17, 1993).

6. *Financial Times*, 1993.

7. Lionel Barber, "Delors Pushes for Monetary 'Fortress Europe'," *Financial Times* (Sept. 19, 1993).

8. Dornbusch, 1996.

9. Thomas Kamm and Cacilie Rohwedder, "Many Europeans Fear Cuts in Social Benefits in One-Currency Plan," *Wall Street Journal* (July 30, 1996).

10. Peter Gumbel and Charles Goldsmith, "EC's Growing Unemployment Provokes Questions About Economic Practices," *Wall Street Journal* (June 18, 1993).

11. Editorial, *Financial Times* (June 21, 1993).

12. Lionel Barber, "The New Hypocrites," *International Economy* (Sept./Oct. 1993).

13. "What Has NAFTA Wrought? Plenty of Trade," *Business Week* (Nov. 21, 1994).

14. See Michael K Frisby, "White House is Divided Over Politics of Trade," *Wall Street Journal* (March 19, 1996).

15. James Brooke, "With a View of One Hemisphere, Latin America is Freeing Its Own Trade," *New York Times* (Dec. 29, 1993).

16. Brooke, 1993.

17. Carla Anne Robbins, "Concerns About NAFTA's Fate Extend to Latin Nations Who Hope to Join," (Washington Insight), *Wall Street Journal* (June 21, 1993), A8(W).

Bibliography

Baldwin, Robert E. 1970. *Nontariff Distortions of International Trade.* Washington, D.C.: Brookings Institution.

———. 1982. "The Political Economy of Protectionism." In Jagdish N. Bhagwati, ed., *Import Competition and Response.* Chicago: University of Chicago Press.

———. 1986. *The Political Economy of U.S. Import Policy.* Cambridge, Ma.: MIT Press.

———. 1987. "The New Protectionism: A Response to Shifts in National Economic Power." In Dominick Salvatore ed., *The New Protectionist Threat to World Welfare.* Amsterdam: Elsevier Science Publishing Company.

Baldwin, Robert E., J. Mutti, and J. David Richardson. 1980. "Welfare Effects on the United States of a Significant Multilateral Tariff Reduction." *Journal of International Economics,*10.

Baldwin, Robert E., and T. S. Thompson. 1984. "The Appropriate Response to Trade Barriers and 'Unfair' Trade Practices in Other Countries." *American Economic Review* 74.

Bandow, Doug *et al.* 1994. *Perpetuating Poverty: The World Bank, the IMF, and the Developing World.* Washington, D.C.: Cato Institute.

Bauer, Peter. 1984. *Reality and Rhetoric: Studies in the Economics of Development.* Cambridge, Ma.: Harvard University Press.

———. 1991. *The Development Frontier: Essays in Applied Economics.* ———. Cambridge, Ma.: Harvard University Press.

Bergsten, C. Fred, and William R. Cline. 1982. *Trade Policy in the 1980s.* Washington, D.C.: Institute for International Economics.

Bhagwati, Jagdish N. 1969. *International Trade.* Harmondsworth, England: Penguin Books.

———. 1983. *International Factor Mobility.* Cambridge, Ma.: MIT Press.

———. 1988. *Protectionism.* Cambridge, Ma.: MIT Press.

———. 1991a. *International Trade and Global Development.* London: Routledge.

———. 1991b. *Political Economy and International Economics.* Cambridge, Ma.: MIT Press.

———. 1991c. *The World Trading System at Risk.* Princeton, N.J.: Princeton University Press.

Bovard, James. 1991. *The Fair Trade Fraud.* New York: St. Martin's Press.

Brock, William A., and Stephen P. Magee. 1980. "Tariff Formation in a Democracy." In John Black and Brian Hindley, eds., *Current Issues in Commercial Policy and Diplomacy.* New York: St. Martin's Press.

Calingaert, Michael. 1996. *European Integration Revisited: Progress, Prospects, and U.S. Interests.* Boulder, Co: Westview Press.

Canto, Victor A.. 1986. *The Determinants and Consequences of Trade Restrictions in the U.S. Economy.* New York: Praeger.

Cooper, Richard N. 1987. "Trade Policy as Foreign Policy." In Robert M. Stern, ed., *U.S. Trade Policies in a Changing World Economy.* Cambridge, Ma.: MIT Press.

Corden, W. Max. 1971. *The Theory of Protection.* Oxford: Clarendon Press.

———. 1984. *The Revival of Protectionism.* New York: Group of Thirty.

———. 1985. *Protection, Growth, and Trade.* Oxford: Blackwell.

———. 1987a. *Protection and Competition in International Trade.* Oxford: Blackwell.

———. 1987b. *Protection and Liberalization.* Washington, D.C.: International Monetary Fund.

———. 1992. *International Trade Theory and Policy: Selected Essays of W. Max Corden.*Economists of the Twentieth Century Series. Brookfield, Vt: Ashgate.

Destler, I. M. 1995. *American Trade Politics.* Third edition. Washington, D.C.: Institute for International Economics; New York: Twentieth Century Fund.

Dixit, Avinash K. 1987. "How Should the United States Respond to Other Countries' Trade Policies?" In Robert M. Stern, ed., *U.S. Trade Policies in a Changing World Economy.* Cambridge, Ma.: MIT Press.

Dornbusch, Rudiger, and Jeffrey A Frankel. 1987. "Macroeconomics and Protection." In Robert M. Stern, ed., *U.S. Trade Policies in a Changing World Economy.* Cambridge, Ma.: MIT Press.

Findlay, Ronald J., and Stanislaw Wellisz. 1983. "Some Aspects of the Political Economy of Trade Restrictions." *Kyklos* 36.

Finger, Michael J. 1993. *Antidumping: How it Works and Who Gets Hurt.* Ann Arbor: The University of Michigan Press.

Friedman, Milton. 1962. *Capitalism and Freedom.* Chicago: University of Chicago Press.

———. 1987. "In Defense of Dumping." *The Commonwealth*, (Aug.).

Friedman, Milton and Rose Friedman. 1980. *Free to Choose: A Personal Statement*. New York: Harcourt Brace & Company.

Goldstein, Judith. 1993. *Ideas, Interests, and American Trade Policy*. Ithaca: Cornell University Press.

Hamada, Koichi et al. 1995. "Behind the US/Japan Trade Conflict." *World Economy* (March).

Harward, David J. . 1995. *International Trade and Regional Economies: The Impacts of European Integration on the United States*. Boulder and Oxford: Harper Collins, Westview.

Hirschman, Albert O. 1958. *The Strategy of Economic Development*. New Haven: Yale University Press.

Hufbauer, Gary C., D. T. Berliner, and K. A. Elliott. 1986. *Trade Protection in the U.S.: 31 Case Studies*. Washington, D.C.: Institute for International Economics.

Hufbauer, Gary C., and Joanna S. Erb. 1984. *Subsidies in International Trade*. Washington, D.C.: Institute for International Economics.

Krauss, Melvyn. 1978. *The New Protectionism*. New York: New York University Press.

———. 1983. *Development Without Aid: Growth, Poverty and Government*. New York: New Press McGraw-Hill Book Company.

———. 1986. *How NATO Weakens The West*. New York: Simon and Schuster.

Krueger, Anne O. et al. 1995. "The Role of the NAFTA Debate in U.S. Trade Policy." *Australian Economic Papers* (June).

Krugman, Paul R., ed., 1986. *Strategic Trade Policy and the New International Economics*. Cambridge, Ma.: MIT Press.

———. 1994a. *International Economics*. Third edition. New York: Harper Collins College Publishers.

———. 1994b. *Peddling Prosperity*. New York: W. W. Norton.

Lawrence, Robert Z. 1984. *Can America Compete?* Washington, D.C.: Brookings Institution.

Lawrence, Robert Z., and Robert E. Litan. 1986. *Saving Free Trade*. Washington: Brookings Institution.

Lindbeck, Assar. 1981. "Disincentive Problems in Developed Countries." *Growth and Entrepreneurship*, International Chamber of Commerce.

———. 1986. "Limits to the Welfare State." *Challenge* (Jan.–Feb).

———. 1987. "Is the Welfare State in Trouble?" *Eastern Economic Journal* (Oct./Dec.).

———. 1988. "Individual Freedom and Welfare State Policy." *European Economic Review* 32.

———. 1993. *The Welfare State: The Selected Essays of Assar Lindbeck*. Brookfield, Vt.: Edward Elgar Publishing Company.

Magee, Stephen P. 1984. "Endogenous Tariff Theory: A Survey." In David C. Colander, ed., *Neoclassical Political Economy*. Cambridge: Ballinger Press.

————. 1987. "The Political Economy of U.S. Protection." In Herbert Gier-
sch, ed., *Free Trade in the World Economy: Towards an Opening of Markets.* Tubingen: J. C. B. Mohr.

Michaely, Michael. 1977. *Theory of Commercial Policy: Trade and Protection.* Chicago: University of Chicago Press.

————. 1985. "The Demand for Protection against Exports of Newly Industrializing Countries." *Journal of Policy Modeling.* 7.

Mundell, Robert A. 1957. "International Trade and Factor Mobility." *American Economic Review* 47.

Myrdal, Gunnar. 1956. *An Internatinal Economy.* New York: Harper &
Brothers.

Nogues, Julio J., Andrzej Olechowski, and L. Alan Winters. 1986. "The
Extent of Nontariff Barriers to Industrial Countries' Imports." *World
Bank Economic Review.* 1.

Ratner, S. 1972. *The Tariff in American History.* New York: Van Nostrand.

Richardson, J. David. 1982. "Trade Adjustment Assistance Under the United
States Trade Act of 1974: An Analytical Examination and Worker Survey." In Jagdish N. Bhagwati, ed., *Import Competition and Response.*
Chicago: University of Chicago Press, for the National Bureau of Economic Research.

Riddell, Roger C. . 1987,. *Foreign Aid Reconsidered.* Baltimore: The Johns
Hopkins University Press.

Roberts, Russell D. 1994. *The Choice.* New York: Prentice Hall.

Saxonhouse, Gary R. 1985. "What's Wrong with Japanese Trade Structure."
Seminar Discussion Paper No. 166. Research Seminar in International
Economics, Dept. of Economics, University of Michigan.

Stern, Robert M., ed. 1987. *U.S. Trade Policies in a Changing World Economy.* Cambridge, Ma.: MIT Press.

Stolper, Wolfgang, and Paul A. Samuelson. 1941. "Protection and Real
Wages." *Review of Economic Studies* 9.

Thurow, Lester C., and Laura D'Andrea Tyson. 1987. "The Economic Black
Hole." *Foreign Policy* 67.

Tower, Edward. 1975. "The Optimum Quota and Retaliation." *Review of
Economic Studies* 42.

Wallis, W. Allen. 1988. *Overview of U.S. Trade Policy.* Washington, D.C.:
U.S. Dept. of State, Bureau of Public Affairs, Office of Public Communi-
cation, Editorial Division.

Walter, Ingo, and Kaj Areskoug. 1981. *International Economics.* Third edition. New York: John Wiley.

Wellisz, Stanislaw, and Ronald Findlay. 1988. "The State and the Invisible
Hand." *Research Observer* 3.

Index